S0-AEJ-810

THE MIMBRES
ART AND ARCHAEOLOGY
by
Jesse Walter Fewkes

Avanyu Publishing Inc.

New Material ©*1989*
AVANYU PUBLISHING, Inc.
P.O. Box 27134
Albuquerque, New Mexico 87125
(505) 243-8485
(505) 266-6128

Library of Congress Cataloging-in-Publication Data

Fewkes, Jesse Walter, 1850-1930.
  The Mimbres: art and archaeology/by Jesse Walter Fewkes.
    p.   cm.
  "A reprint of three papers . . . published by the Smithsonian Institution
between 1914 and 1924."
  ISBN 0-936755-10-5 paperback. ISBN 0-936755-11-3 hardback.
  1. Mogollon culture. 2. Indians of North America–New Mexico–Mimbres
River Valley–Pottery. 3. Indians of North America–New Mexico–Mimbres
River Valley–Antiquities. 4. Mimbres River Valley (N.M.)–Antiquities. 5. New
Mexico–Antiquities. I. Title.
E99.M76F48 1989
978.9'692–dc20   89-6869
                                                                                    CIP

All rights reserved. No portion of this publication may be reproduced or transmit-
ted in any form or by any means, electronic or mechanical, including photocopying,
recording, or any information storage or retrieval system without permission in
writing from the publisher.

Third printing 1993

Avanyu Publishing Inc.

THE MIMBRES
ART AND ARCHAEOLOGY
by
Jesse Walter Fewkes

A reprint of three essays authored
by Jesse Walter Fewkes and published
by The Smithsonian Institution
between 1914 and 1924.

With an Introduction
by J. J. Brody,
Professor of Art and Art History,
University of New Mexico.

Avanyu Publishing Inc.

ACKNOWLEDGEMENTS

We wish to thank the School of American Research, Santa Fe, NM, and the University of New Mexico Press, Albuquerque, NM for permitting use of maps and photographs previously published in *Mimbres Painted Pottery* by J. J. Brody. Appreciation is extended also to The Heard Museum, Phoenix, AZ, and the United States National Museum, Smithsonian Institution, Washington, D.C. for permitting use of previously published photographs from the same referenced work.

The maps on the endpapers have been reproduced without change from *Mimbres Painted Pottery* by J. J. Brody, with permission of the School of American Research and the University of New Mexico Press.

Avanyu Publishing Inc.

CONTENTS

Avanyu Publishing Inc.

Avanyu Publishing Inc.

PREFACE

Avanyu Publishing is pleased to offer as its first book on pottery a reprint of three essays by J. Walter Fewkes on the magnificent work of the Mimbres Indians. We at Avanyu Publishing feel it is proper to select the most artistic of the prehistoric potters for our first book on pottery.

The Mimbres Indians remained basically unknown and unstudied by scholars until Jesse Walter Fewkes published his essays in the early 1920s. Yet, very little interest was shown between the 1920s and 1970s, a half century of indifference. By the 1970s gravediggers and pot-hunters had discovered the enormous profit to be made from sales of Mimbres pottery to collectors. New laws have hopefully put a stop to such needless and reckless destruction of these prehistoric sites.

For three years Avanyu Publishing Inc. had been seeking original copies of these articles from the Smithsonian's Miscellaneous Collections. Now that all three have been found, we bring them together for the archaeologist, the anthropologist, the student, the scholar, and the collector. We are very fortunate to have had Dr. J. J. Brody write an accurate historical and aesthetic overview to these articles. We gratefully acknowledge Dr. Brody's assistance, especially in light of severe time restraints.

It is our hope and intent that republishing these three Fewkes essays, supplemented with the new essay by Dr. J. J. Brody, will bring to the attention of a new group of scholars and collectors information about the outstanding artistic talent of the Mimbres.

We now have reprinted books in the fields of Pueblo Indian religious ceremonies, Navajo weavings, reservation traders, and early mail order catalogs. We have been pleased with the positive response to the titles we have

Avanyu Publishing Inc.

selected to bring back into print. All of our books on Navajo weaving and Navajo reservation traders have been received with great enthusiasm. The two books about Zuni which we co-published with Rio Grande Press and the one published under our own logo have been as popular with the Zuni Indians as with non-Indian readers.

We anticipate that our newly released book, *A Little History of the Navajos* by Oscar H. Lipps, will be received with equal enthusiasm. It is a concise and accurate history of the Navajo Indians as they were between 1860 and 1900, giving a white man's view of their history, pastoral existence, arts and crafts, mythology, ceremonies, and religion, based upon his personal experiences. Mr. Lipps' narrative examines both the positive and negative influences of the white man on the Navajo's life and culture. Such insight into the history of the Navajo is enlightening to readers of all backgrounds, especially to those who have, themselves, dealt with the Navajo.

We have a number of subjects and titles in mind for future release, but we encourage our readers to feed us ideas of out of print books they would like to see available again.

Alexander E. Anthony, Jr.   J. Brent Ricks

Avanyu Publishing Inc.

INTRODUCTION

Jesse Walter Fewkes (1850-1930)

Between the years 1914 and 1924 the three essays that are reprinted here introduced Mimbres art to our century. The remarkable paintings on pottery by those ancient and until then unnamed southwestern people had only recently been rediscovered, having been hidden from all human knowledge for almost 800 years. Word about the art spread slowly in that era before mass media. At first, only a few people living in southwestern New Mexico were aware of it, then it became known to a handful of specialists, presumably readers of *Smithsonian Miscellaneous Collections,* and it only began to reach a somewhat larger audience about the time of World War II.

J. Walter Fewkes tells us in a matter-of-fact way of his introduction to Mimbres art. Late in 1913 E. D. Osborn of Deming, New Mexico sent a letter and photographs of Mimbres pottery to the Bureau of American Ethnology (BAE) of the Smithsonian Institution in Washington, D.C. where Fewkes was senior ethnologist. We must read between the lines to sense the excitement created by those pictures for, hardly six months and a long train ride later, he was in Deming visiting collectors of Mimbres art, acquiring specimens for the Smithsonian, and investigating ruins of Mimbres villages and their rock art sites in the Florida Mountains, on Cook's Peak, and along the Mimbres River valley. He does not tell us how long he stayed, but whether it was a week or a month, he was a very busy man for he covered

Avanyu Publishing Inc.

1

Fewkes: 1923, Fig. 10.

Fewkes: 1924, Fig. 34.

hundreds of square miles of rugged terrain in desert heat at a horse's pace.

Fewkes was sixty-four years old in 1914 and his decision to make the arduous trip could not have been taken lightly. But there were few people more familiar than he with southwestern archaeology nor were there many better able to make informed judgements about the potential significance of the pictures that Osborn had sent. He knew that the trip to Mimbres country was going to be interesting, and it might even have been self-indulgent for him to make it–after all it got him away from Washington and back into the field. There was nothing selfish, however, in his decision to immediately prepare a thoroughly researched report describing Mimbres art and placing it as accurately as was then possible in archaeological, ethnographic, and historical contexts. Within six months of his return to Washington his first Mimbres paper, *Archeology of the Lower Mimbres Valley, New Mexico,* was in press.

He became head of the BAE in 1918, but the administrative load slowed him down not at all for he continued field work (mostly in the Mesa Verde region where he seems to have invented campfire talks for the National Park Service) and produced thirty professional papers during the next eight years. Bad health forced his retirement in 1928 and he died two years later. He seems never to have returned to the Mimbres valley. His other major papers on Mimbres art, published in 1923 and 1924, were based upon collections made by Osborn, Harriet and Cornelius Cosgrove, R.E. Eisele, and other amateur

Fewkes: 1924, Fig. 45.

Fewkes: 1924, Fig. 47.

archaeologists. As in the earlier work, the later papers combine descriptions of Mimbres paintings with interpretations of their archaeological and ethnographic significance. Some of his later judgements differ from those made a decade earlier.

Those familiar with Fewkes' bibliography will not be surprised at his energy nor at the quality, depth, or limitations of these reports. He was among the most prolific scientific authors of his own–or any other–time, and many of his papers and monographs remain standard references almost a century after their original publication. Several, (including at least one of this threesome), periodically emerge in new editions like mushrooms on a wet forest floor. Most of his output was based on field work, and, as happened with the Mimbres, some of that work was brief and in the nature of a reconnaissance. Perhaps for that reason his reports often acknowledge important contributions made by collaborators and local amateurs.

He was both an archaeologist and ethnologist who typified an Americanist view of prehistory as "the ethnology of the past." Most remarkably, considering his vast output and great influence, he did no anthropological work until he was almost forty. He was trained at Harvard University in natural history and marine geology as a student of the formidable Louis Agassiz. He earned his doctorate there in 1877 and in little more than a decade published sixty-nine papers in his chosen field. He first showed an interest in anthropology in 1888

Avanyu Publishing Inc.

3

Fewkes: 1923, Fig. 9.   Fewkes: 1923, Fig. 29.

and began ethnographic field work the next year. Throughout a long and distinguished career in anthropology his training as a natural historian was always evident.

At first he worked most intensely amongst the Hopi pueblos of northeastern Arizona. He focused upon their mythic traditions and ceremonial life, with the masked dances and related arts of the Kachina Societies of special interest to him. Considering both his original profession and the fact that historic sources of the Homeric legends had only recently been demonstrated, it was only reasonable for him to assume that the poetic metaphors of Hopi oral traditions were based upon historic events. Consequently, his early archaeological work was inspired by a search for evidence to support literal interpretations of Hopi myth. Similar literal expectations, objective descriptions, and a Hopi orientation color his interpretations of Mimbres art.

The Mimbres Culture

The Mimbres people were a branch of the Mogollon culture and their art was related in many ways to that of their Hohokam and Anasazi neighbors. Yet Fewkes wrote of the Mimbres as a river rather than a people, of the Mogollon as a mountain range rather than a culture, and the words Anasazi and Hohokam do not appear in any of these papers. The outlines of southwestern

Avanyu Publishing Inc.

Fewkes: 1923, Fig. 119.

Fewkes: 1924, Fig. 27.

prehistory were sketchy in 1914 and still unclear a decade later. It was not until 1927 that archaeologists reached broad agreement on terminology, and on an outline of the culture history of the northern part of the southwest, which we now call the Anasazi district. The southern parts remained problematic until the late 1930s when culture sequences were first proposed for what we now call the Mogollon and Hohokam regions. The Mimbres people thereafter were considered to be one of several branches of Mogollon culture.

A great deal of scientific archaeology was done in the Mimbres area during the decade of the 1920s. Some, perhaps most of it, was stimulated by Fewkes' 1914 publication which demonstrated the need to clarify the prehistory of the southern southwest. Then, very little happened for forty years until about 1972 when a new, fruitful, and still on-going campaign of archaeological investigations began. Excavations by local, amateur archaeologists and pot collectors never ended, but must be distinguished from the entirely destructive and sometimes criminal looting by professional pot-hunters that started in the 1960s when Mimbres art first became a valued commodity on the world art market.

Among institutions involved in Mimbres archaeological investigations during the 1920s were the School of American Research, Museum of New Mexico, Peabody Museum of Harvard University, Beloit College, University of Minne-

Avanyu Publishing Inc.

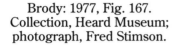

Brody: 1977, Fig. 167.
Collection, Heard Museum;
photograph, Fred Stimson.

Fewkes: 1923, Fig. 1.

sota, and Southwest Museum in Los Angeles. Each was motivated to some degree by a desire to collect Mimbres art, but all published monographs and papers that placed the art in historic and social contexts. The Mimbres publications of Wesley Bradfield, Harriet and Cornelius Cosgrove, and Paul Nesbitt were especially important, building upon, refining, and modifying Fewkes' pioneering work. They provided data bases and contextual backgrounds for the much later interpretive and art historical studies of Mimbres art by Fred Kabotie, Pat Carr, and myself.

The more recent archaeological programs are indebted to those of earlier times but are far more refined both technically and theoretically. In every case now the investigations are motivated by intellectual concerns rather than the desire to build collections. Special importance must be placed on the work of the Mimbres Foundation, Texas A&M University, and the many consequent publications by Steven LeBlanc, Harry Shafer, Roger Anyon, and their colleagues. Perhaps the most valuable contribution to the study of Mimbres art is Catherine Scott's typology of its style changes. The last two decades have greatly expanded our knowledge of the Mimbres culture and our ability to interpret Mimbres art.

Avanyu Publishing Inc.

Brody: 1977, Fig. 168.
Collection, Western New
Mexico University Museum;
photograph, Fred Stimson.

Fewkes: 1924, Fig. 2.

Mimbres Art

Most of the drawings published by Fewkes are of Mimbres Classic paintings (Style III in Scott's terminology), dating from the early 1000s to about 1150. A very few, reproduced on these pages, (1923: figs. 9, 10; 1924: figs. 34, 45, 47) appear to be late Mimbres Boldface pictures of the tenth century (Style II). No ninth century early Boldface paintings (Style I) are shown. Fewkes could hardly have had a clear idea about either chronology or the stylistic history of Mimbres art. He was limited, first, by the virtual absence in his sample of early examples that might have suggested developmental sequences to him; second, by the general absence of contextual information about most of the pictures; and third, by the total absence of a comprehensive theory concerning the culture history of the region or the people who had made the art.

He had other, more personal limitations. He shared with virtually all later investigators the desire to identify Mimbres painted images with real world animals. And, like everyone else, he was occasionally embarrassed because Mimbres artists very often were deliberately ambiguous in their representations. Even Fewkes, the trained naturalist, identifies a frog as a turtle, and insects as birds (1923: figs. 29, 119). Of greater interest was his curious

Avanyu Publishing Inc.

Brody: 1977, Fig. 160.
Collection, Southwest
Museum;
Photograph, Fred Stimson.

Fewkes: 1923, Fig. 41.

tolerance for morphological *errors* such as the creature he identifies as a bat despite its feathered wing (1924: fig. 27). His insistence upon a literal, worldly interpretation of Mimbres iconography may have blinded him to its rich metaphors which hide clues to mythic traditions that most likely were comparable to those he found so stimulating at Hopi.

Most Mimbres paintings and all that were known to Fewkes are on the inner surfaces of hemispherical bowls that are about two and a half times wider than they are deep. They are portable, kinetic, and have no fixed vertical axis–no top or bottom. All two-dimensional images of them must distort their visual qualities, especially if the vertical axis is made static as on a printed page. Compare the photograph of a painting acquired by The Heard Museum in 1952 (Brody 1977: fig. 167) with a drawing of it (printed backwards in Fewkes 1923: fig. 1).

When reproduced two-dimensionally, the focal point of a painting often appears to be in the center of its hemispherical picture space even though it may actually be on the upper walls. Compare the photograph of a painting donated to the Western New Mexico University Museum in 1973 (Brody 1977: fig. 168) with a drawing of it in Fewkes 1924 (fig. 2); or the photograph of a

Avanyu Publishing Inc.

Brody: 1977, Fig. 104.
Collection, United States
National Museum;
photograph, USNM.

Fewkes: 1924, Fig. 10.

painting acquired by the Southwest Museum in 1947 (Brody 1977: fig. 160) with its drawing in Fewkes 1923 (fig. 41).

Other distortions occur, as when photographs of painted bowls are flattened by being taken head-on with no shadows. There are trade-offs. A drawing may disguise unique linear values, make parabolic lines appear to be straight, and lose other dynamic qualities and yet clarify the painted image by deleting the stains, breaks, and cracks that make it difficult to read. Compare the photograph of a painting acquired in 1923 for the U.S. National Museum (Brody 1977: fig. 104) with its drawing in Fewkes 1924 (fig. 10).

Some of the drawings published here had impacts that may have been unanticipated. Julian Martinez of San Ildefonso Pueblo seems to have had immediate access to the 1923 and 1924 monographs for there was hardly any time lag between their publication and his use of images from them on the pottery of his wife, Maria Martinez. One painting, (1923: fig. 120), acquired by The Heard Museum in 1952 (Brody 1977: fig. 75) became the prototype for the most popular San Ildefonso design of the modern era. Its publication as a flat image may have suggested the common placement on flat dishes and the exterior of globular jars. In the 1950s the three volumes became source books

Avanyu Publishing Inc.

Brody: 1977, Fig. 75.
Collection, Heard Museum;
photograph, Fred Stimson.

Fewkes: 1923, Fig. 120.

for a revival of Mimbres designs at Acoma Pueblo, again on a variety of shapes that Mimbres pottery painters rarely, if ever, used.

It sometimes happens in the best of all scholarly worlds that publications, like works of art, take on a life of their own and are used and re-used in unimaginable ways by unknown audiences. J. Walter Fewkes somehow aligned himself in an appropriate way with Mimbres art–as he did also with the art of the Hopi–and by a combination of sensitivity and association, cut himself a slice of immortality or the next thing to it.

J. J. Brody, Professor
Department of Art and Art History
University of New Mexico

Avanyu Publishing Inc.

BIBLIOGRAPHY

Anyon, Roger and Steven A. LeBlanc. *The Galaz Ruin: A Prehistoric Mimbres Village in Southwestern New Mexico.* Maxwell Museum of Anthropology and University of New Mexico Press, Albuquerque, 1984.

Bradfield, Wesley. *Cameron Creek Village, a Site in the Mimbres Area in Grant County, New Mexico.* School of American Research, Santa Fe, 1929.

Brody, J. J. *Mimbres Painted Pottery.* University of New Mexico, Albuquerque, and School of American Research, Santa Fe, 1977.

Brody, J. J., Steven LeBlanc, and Catherine J. Scott. *Mimbres Pottery: Ancient Art of the American Southwest.* Hudson Hills Press, N.Y., 1983.

Carr, Patricia. *Mimbres Mythology.* Southwestern Studies Monograph, no. 56. University of Texas, El Paso, 1979.

Cosgrove, Harriet S. and Cornelius B. *The Swarts Ruin, A Typical Mimbres Site in Southwestern New Mexico.* Papers of the Peabody Museum of American Archeology and Ethnology, Harvard University 15 (1), 1932.

Hough, Walter. "Jesse Walter Fewkes." *American Anthropologist* 33:92-97. 1931.

Avanyu Publishing Inc.

Kabotie, Fred. *Designs from the Ancient Mimbrenos with a Hopi Interpretation.* Graborn Press, San Francisco, 1949.

LeBlanc, Steven A. *The Mimbres People: Ancient Painters of the American Southwest.* Thames and Hudson, London, 1983.

Nesbitt, Paul H. *The Ancient Mimbrenos, Based on Investigations at the Mattocks Ruin, Mimbres Valley, New Mexico.* Logan Museum Bulletin 4, Beloit College, Beloit, Wisconsin, 1931.

Shafer, Harry J., A. J. Taylor, and Steve J. Usrey. *Archaeology of the NAN Ranch Ruin, Grant County, New Mexico: A Preliminary Report.* Anthropology Laboratory Special Series 3. Texas A&M University, College Station, 1979.

Swanton, J. R. and F. H. Roberts, Jr. "Jesse Walter Fewkes." *Smithsonian Institution Annual Report for 1920,* 609-619. 1931.

Avanyu Publishing Inc.

ARCHEOLOGY OF THE LOWER MIMBRES
VALLEY, NEW MEXICO

Avanyu Publishing Inc.

SMITHSONIAN MISCELLANEOUS COLLECTIONS

VOLUME 63, NUMBER 10

ARCHEOLOGY OF THE LOWER MIMBRES VALLEY, NEW MEXICO

(WITH EIGHT PLATES)

BY

J. WALTER FEWKES

(PUBLICATION 2316)

CITY OF WASHINGTON
PUBLISHED BY THE SMITHSONIAN INSTITUTION
1914

The Lord Baltimore Press
BALTIMORE, MD., U. S. A.

ARCHEOLOGY OF THE LOWER MIMBRES VALLEY, NEW MEXICO

By J. WALTER FEWKES

(With Eight Plates)

Introduction

Evidences of the existence of a prehistoric population in the Lower Mimbres Valley, New Mexico, have been accumulating for many years, but there is little definite knowledge of its culture and kinship. It is taken for granted, by some writers, that the ancient people of this valley lived in habitations resembling the well-known terraced dwellings called pueblos, many of which are still inhabited along the Rio Grande; but this theory presupposes that there was a close likeness in the prehistoric architectural remains of northern and southern New Mexico. It may be said that while there were many likenesses in their culture, the prehistoric inhabitants of these two regions possessed striking differences, notably in their architecture, their mortuary customs, and the symbolic ornamentation of their pottery.

As the former inhabitants of the Mimbres Valley have left no known descendants of pure blood, and as there is a scarcity of historical records, we must rely on a study of archeological remains to extend our knowledge of the subject. Much data of this kind has already been lost, for while from time to time numerous instructive relics of this ancient culture have been found, most of these objects have been treated as " curios " and given away to be carried out of the country, and thus lost to science. Some of these relics belong to a type that it is difficult to duplicate. For instance, it is particularly to be regretted that the numerous votive offerings to water gods, including fossil bones, found when the " sacred spring " at Faywood near the Mimbres was cleaned out, have not been studied and described by some competent archeologist. The arrowheads, lance-points, and " cloud-blowers " from this spring are particularly fine examples, the most important objects of the collection being now in the cabinet of Mrs. A. R. Graham of Chicago.[1]

---

[1] In a letter to Professor W. H. Holmes, published in his paper, " Flint Implements and Fossil Remains from a Sulphur Spring at Afton, Indian Terri-

The valley of the Mimbres has never been regarded as favorable to archeological studies, but has practically been overlooked, possibly because of the more attractive fields in the regions to the north and west, so that only very meager accounts have been published.[1]

The present article, which is a preliminary report on an archeological excursion into this valley in May and June, 1914, is an effort to add to existing knowledge of the archeology of the valley. During this reconnaissance the author obtained by excavation and purchase a collection of prehistoric objects which have added desirable exhibition material to the collections in the U. S. National Museum.[2]

HISTORICAL

The recorded history of the inhabitants of the Mimbres is brief. One of the earliest descriptions of the valley, in English, is found in Bartlett's " Personal Narrative," published in 1854. In his account of a trip to the copper mines at the present Santa Rita, Bartlett records seeing a herd of about twenty black-tailed deer, turkeys and other game birds, antelopes, bears, and fine trout in the streams. He

tory," Mr. A. R. Graham gives an instructive account of cleaning out the Faywood Hot Springs where he found the following relics: (1) parts of skulls and bones of several human beings; (2) over fifty spearheads and arrowheads of every shape and style of workmanship, the spearheads being valuable for their size and symmetry; (3) nine large warclubs made of stone; (4) a large variety of teeth of animals as well as large bones of extinct animals; (5) the most interesting relics are ten stone pipes from four to seven inches in length; (6) flint hatchet and a stone hammer, together with stones worn flat from use; beads made of vegetable seed and bird bones; part of two Indian bows with which was found a quiver in which was quite a bunch of long, coarse black hair that was soon lost after being dried.—Amer. Anthrop., n. s., vol. 4, pp. 126, 127.

[1] The Santa Rita mines early attracted the conquistadors looking for gold, and were worked in ancient times by the Spaniards, the ores obtained finding an outlet along a road down the valley to the city of Chihuahua. The prehistoric people also mined native Mimbres copper, and probably obtained from these mines and from those in Cook's Range, the native copper from which were made the hawk-bells sometimes found in Arizona and New Mexico. From these localities also were derived fragments of float copper often found in Southwestern ruins and commonly ascribed to localities in Mexico. From here came also a form of primitive stone mauls used in early days of the working of the mines.

[2] The National Museum had nothing from the Lower Mimbres before this addition, although it has a few specimens, without zoic designs, from Fort Bayard, in the Upper Mimbres. The latter are figured by Dr. Hough, Bull. 87, U. S. National Museum.

says very little, however, about antiquities, although he passed through a region where there are still several mounds indicating ruins. Bartlett writes (*op. cit.*, vol. 1, p. 218) :

On April 29, hearing that there were traces of an ancient Indian settlement about half a mile distant, Dr. Webb went over to examine it, while we were getting ready to move. He found a good deal of broken pottery, all of fine texture. Some of it bore traces of red, black, and brown colors. He also found a stone mortar about eight inches in diameter. I have since understood that this was the seat of one of the earliest Spanish missions; but it was abandoned more than a century ago, and no traces remain but a few heaps of crumbling adobes, which mark the site of its dwellings.

This ruin was situated near the Rio Grande, twenty-three miles from Mule Spring, on the road to the Mimbres. Bartlett does not tell us how he learned that this was an early mission site, but from the pottery it is evident that it was an "ancient Indian settlement."

After having examined the configuration of the country through which Bartlett passed, and having compared it with statements in his description, the present writer thinks that Bartlett camped on May 1, 1853, near the Oldtown ruin and that the place then bore the name Pachetehu. This camp was nineteen [eighteen?] miles from Cow Spring and thirteen miles from the copper mines.

Bartlett records that he found, near his camp, " several old Indian encampments with their wigwams standing and about them fragments of pottery." Although not very definite, these references might apply either to the Oldtown ruin and some others a few miles up the river, or to more modern Apache dwellings.

Mr. F. S. Dellenbaugh claims that Coronado, in 1540, passed through the valley of the Mimbres on his way to Cibola, and that this place was somewhere in this region, instead of at Zuñi, as taught by Bandelier and others. The present writer recognizes that the question of the route of Coronado is one for historical experts to answer, but believes that new facts regarding the ruins in the Mimbres may have a bearing upon this question and are desirable. While it can no longer be said in opposition to Dellenbaugh's theory that there are no ruins in the valley between Deming and the Mexican border, we have not yet been able to discover whether the ruins here described were or were not inhabited in 1540.

The fragmentary notice of the ruins in the Upper Mimbres and Silver City region by Bandelier is one of the best thus far published, although he denies the existence of ruins now known in the great stretch of desert from Deming to the Mexican boundary. Regarding the ruins on the Upper Mimbres, Bandelier writes:[1]

Toward this center of drainage the aboriginal villages on the Rio Mimbres have gravitated as far south nearly as the flow of water is now permanent. They are very abundant on both sides of the stream, wherever the high over-hanging plateaux have left any habitable and tillable space; they do not seem to extend east as far as Cook's Range, but have penetrated into the Sierra Mimbres farther north, as far as twenty miles from the river eastward. . . . . The total number of ruins scattered as far north as Hincks' Ranch on a stretch of about thirty miles along the Mimbres in the valley proper, I estimate at about sixty. . . . . I have not seen a village whose population I should estimate at over one hundred, and the majority contained ten. They were built of rubble in mud or adobe mortar, the walls usually thin, with overwings, and a fireplace in the corner, formed by a recess bulging out of a wall. Toward the lower end of the permanent water course, the ruins are said to be somewhat extensive.

Professor U. Francis Duff, in an article on the "Ruins of the Mimbres Valley,"[2] adds a number of new sites to those mentioned above and contributes important additions to our knowledge of the prehistoric culture of the valley.

Dr. Walter Hough, who compiled from Bandelier and Duff, and made use of unpublished information furnished by Professor De Lashmutt and others, enumerates twenty-seven ruins in the Silver City and Mimbres region to which he assigns the numbers 147-174. Many more ruins[3] might have been included in this list, but it is not the author's purpose, at this time, to mention individual pueblo sites but rather to call attention to the evidences of ruins in the Lower Mimbres Valley as an introduction to the study of pottery there collected. The ruin from which the majority of the bowls here considered were obtained does not appear to have been mentioned by Bandelier, Duff, or Hough.

The last-mentioned author makes the following reference to figures on the pottery from the Mimbres region: " The decoration is mainly geometric. From the Mimbres he [Professor De Lashmutt] has seen a realistic design resembling a grasshopper, and from Fort Bayard another representing a four-legged creature. Mrs. Owen has a

[1] Archæological Institute of America, American Series, vol. 4, Final Report, Part 2, pp. 356, 357.

[2] American Antiquarian, vol. 24, p. 397, 1902.

[3] Bandelier (op. cit., p. 357) speaks of sixty ruins in a small section thirty miles along the river.

specimen from Fort Bayard bearing what is described as a 'fish design.'"[1] Dr. Hough likewise points out that

pottery from some sites [ruins] is also different from that of any other [Pueblo] region and is affiliated, in some respects, with that of the Casas Grandes, in Chihuahua which lies in the low foot-hills of Sierra Madre. This is especially true in reference to fragments of yellow ware found here [the Florida Mountains] which in both form and color of decoration is manifestly like that of Casas Grandes.[2]

The latest and thus far the most important contribution to our knowledge of the prehistoric people of the Mimbres we owe to Mr. C. L. Webster, who has published several articles on the antiquities of the Upper Mimbres, in " The Archæological Bulletin." He has made known several new village sites along the valley and has mentioned, for the first time, details regarding Mimbres ruins and the objects found in them. Practically nothing has thus far been recorded on the antiquities of the region immediately about Deming, nor of those south of that important railroad center to the Mexican border.

In an article on " Some Burial Customs Practiced by the Ancient People of the Southwest,"[3] Mr. Webster describes and figures a human burial on the Lower Mimbres not far from the " Military Post," situated near Oldtown. It was found in the plain some distance from any indications of prehistoric settlement. He says :

An exploration of it [a burial] revealed that originally a circular excavation, perhaps three feet in diameter and slightly more in depth, had been made in the ground ; and afterwards the body placed at the bottom of this excavation in a sitting posture with the knees somewhat drawn up and arms to the side, and then a very large earthen olla, of a reddish color, was set over it, bottom side up, thus protecting it from the earth which was afterwards thrown in, filling up the excavation.

Mr. Webster shows that the Mimbres aborigines did not always bury their dead in a contracted or seated posture. He speaks also of intramural or house burials in the valley of Rio Sapillo, a tributary of the Upper Gila, not far from the source of the Mimbres. In this region he dug down in one of the central rooms of a ruin about three feet below the surface, where he says (p. 73) :

Near the bottom of this excavation hard red clay was encountered, which on opening up proved to contain the well-preserved skeleton of an adult person

---

[1] Bull. 35, Bur. Amer. Ethn., p. 83. See also an article subsequently published on the Culture of the Ancient Pueblos of the Upper Gila River Region, Bull. 87, 1913, U. S. National Museum, in which several bowls with geometrical designs from Fort Bayard are figured.

[2] Bandelier found that Mimbres pottery resembles that of several regions, including Casas Grandes.

[3] The Archæological Bulletin, vol. 3, No. 3, p. 70.

which had been placed at length on its back with arms at its side. Over the face of this one [human burial] had been placed a rather large shallow dish, through the bottom of which a hole about the size of a five cent piece, or a little larger, had been carefully drilled. This hole was so located as to occupy a position between the eyes when placed over the face. This body was resting on a bed of red clay like that which had covered it. Near the first body was a second body which had been buried in exactly the same way, and had a similar perforated dish over its face. Under this first or upper tier of bodies a second tier of bodies was discovered which had been buried exactly the same way as the upper tier—each one resting separate and alone, though near together, each one tightly enveloped in stiff red clay.

All the vessels placed over the faces showed the action of fire, and it was plain to be seen they had once been used in cooking. . . . . The method practised here was to first spread down a layer of red plastic clay, then lay the body upon it, place the perforated dish over the face and finally plaster all with a covering of the same clay. This same method was followed in every case observed.

SITES OF RUINS IN THE LOWER MIMBRES VALLEY

The portion of the Sierra Madre plateau called Lower Mimbres, or Antelope Valley, extends from where the Mimbres sinks below the surface at Oldtown to Lake Palomas in Mexico, twenty-five miles south of Deming. According to some writers this region has no prehistoric ruins, but several of the beautiful specimens described and figured in the present article came from this valley, and there are doubtless many others, equally instructive, still awaiting the spade of the archeologist. The purest form of the Mimbres prehistoric culture is found in the lower or southern part of this plain, but it extends into the hills far up the Mimbres almost to its source.

The plateau on which the prehistoric Mimbres culture developed is geographically well marked, and distinguished from other regions of the Southwest geographically and biologically, facts reflected in human culture. The cultural gateway is open to migrations from the south rather than from the east, north, or west.

The evidences drawn from the poor preservation of the walls of the ruins, and the paucity of historical references to them, instead of indicating absence of a prehistoric population suggest the existence of a very ancient culture that had been replaced by wandering Apache tribes years before the advent of the Spaniards. Chronologically the prehistoric people belongs to an older epoch than the Pueblo, and its culture resembles that which antedated the true Pueblos.[1]

---

[1] During the author's stay in Deming he was much indebted to Dr. S. D. Swope for many kindnesses, among which was an opportunity to study his valuable collection, now in the high school of that city. He was also greatly

The ruins here considered do not belong to the same type as those of the Lower Gila and Salt, although they may be contemporaneous with them, and may have been inhabited at the same time as those on the Casas Grandes River in northern Chihuahua. Not regarded as belonging to the same series of ruins as those on the Upper Gila and Salt rivers, they are not designated numerically with them.

Although the indications of an ancient prehistoric occupancy of the Mimbres are so numerous, they are so indistinct and have been so little studied that any attempt here to include all of them would be premature. Remains of human occupancy occur in the plain about Deming, and can be traced northward along the river east and west into the mountains, and south into Mexico.

The author has observed many evidences of former settlements along the Upper Mimbres which have not yet been recorded. The indications are, as a rule, inconspicuous, appearing on the surface of the ground in the form of rows of stones or bases of house walls, fragments of pottery, and broken stone implements, such as metates and manos. These sites are commonly called " Indian graves," skeletons often having been excavated from the enclosures outlined by former house walls. There are also evidences of prehistoric ditches at certain points along the Mimbres, showing that the ancients irrigated their small farms.

No attempt is made here to consider all the ruins of the Mimbres or of the Antelope plain in the immediate neighborhood of Deming, but only those that have been visited, mainly ruins from which the objects here described were obtained.

Although few of the walls of the ancient buildings rise high above ground, they can be readily traced in several places. From remains that were examined it appears that the walls were sometimes built of stone laid in mortar and plastered on the inside, or of adobe strengthened at the base with stones and supported by logs, a few of which have been found in place upright. No differentiation of sacred and secular rooms was noticed, and no room could be identified as belonging to the type called kiva. The floors of the rooms were made of " caleche," hardened by having been tramped down ; the fireplace was placed in one corner, on the floor, and the entrance to the room was probably at one side. To all intents and purposes these dwellings were probably not unlike those fragile wattle-walled structures found

---

aided by Mr. E. D. Osborn and several other citizens, and takes this opportunity to thank all who rendered assistance in his studies. The photographs reproduced in the present paper were made by Mr. Osborn.

very generally throughout the prehistoric Southwest, and supposed to antedate the communal dwellings or pueblos of northern New Mexico.

The two aboriginal sites in the Mimbres Valley that have yielded the majority of the specimens here figured and described are the Old-town ruin and the Osborn ruin, a small village site twelve miles south of Deming and four miles west of the Florida Mountains. There are some differences in general appearance and variations in the minor archeological objects from these two localities, but it is supposed that specimens from both indicate a closely related, if not identical, culture area.

About a year ago Mr. E. D. Osborn, of Deming, who had commenced excavation in these ruins,[1] obtained from them a considerable collection of pottery and other objects. His letters on the subject and his photographs of the pottery, sent to the Bureau of American Ethnology, first led the author to visit southern New Mexico to investigate the archeology of the Mimbres.

VILLAGE SITE NEAR OSBORN RANCH [2]

A few extracts from Mr. Osborn's letters regarding this site form a fitting introduction to a description of the sites and the objects from them:

At the present time [December 8, 1913] the nearest permanent water to this place [site of the cemetery] is either the Palomas Lake in Mexico, twenty-five miles south, or thirty miles north, where the Mimbres River sinks into the earth. . . . . This supposed Pueblo site is situated upon a low sandy ridge which at this point makes a right-angle bend, one part running south and the other west from the angle. The top and sides of the ridge, also the "flat" enclosed between the areas of the ridge, to the extent of about an acre, is littered all over with fragments, charcoal and debris containing bones to the depth of from one to three feet. There are also a great many broken metates and grinding stones. . . . . In digging on top of this ridge, near the angle, we occasionally found what appeared to have been adobe wall foundations, but not sufficiently large to determine the size or shape of any building. In digging on the ridge a few stone implements were found, including one fine stone axe, stone paint pots and mortars, and a few arrowheads, also two bone awls and a few shell beads and bracelets, the last all broken. The only article of wood was the stump of a large cedar post full of knots, badly decayed; it had been burned off two or three inches below the surface of the ground. The cemetery was found on the inner slope of the angle facing the southwest. . . . . In a

---

[1] Specimens were also found by Mr. Osborn at the Byron Ranch ruin, at the Black Mountain site, and elsewhere.

[2] This is the ruin called Osborn ruin in subsequent descriptions.

large proportion of cases the body was placed upon its back, feet drawn up against the body, knees higher than the head; sometimes the head was face up and sometimes it was pressed forward so the top of the head was uppermost. In other interments the body was extended its full length with face up. A large majority of the skulls had a bowl[1] inverted over them, though I judge twenty per cent were without any bowl. . . . . In a great many instances after the body had been placed in the grave with bowl over the head, a little soil was filled in, and about one foot of adobe mud was added and tramped down then filled up with soil. This adobe mud is almost like rock, making it difficult to dig up the bowl without smashing it. . . . . No article of any kind except the bowl over the head was found in any grave. In one case a bowl was found with a skull under it and under that skull was another bowl and another skull.

Few evidences of upright walls of buildings are found at or near this site. The surface of the ground in places rises into low mounds devoid of bushes, which grow sparingly in the immediate neighborhood, but no trees of any considerable size were noticed in the vicinity. Before work began at this place the only signs of former occupancy by aborigines, besides walls, were a few broken fragments of ancient pottery, metates, or a burnt stump protruding here and there from the ground. None of the house walls projected very high above the surface of the ground. Excavations in the floors of rooms at this point yielded so many human skeletons that the place was commonly referred to as a cemetery, but all indications support the conclusion that it was probably a village site with intramural interments.

The human burials here found had knees flexed or drawn to the breast in the " contracted " position, sometimes with the face turned eastward. The skeletons were sometimes found in shallow graves, but often were buried deeply below the surface. Almost without exception the crania had bowls fitted over them like caps. The graves as a rule are limited to soft ground, the bowls resting on undisturbed sand devoid of human remains. In some instances there appears to have been a hardened crust of clay above the remains, possibly all that is left of the floor of a dwelling. The indications are that here, as elsewhere, the dead were buried under the floors of dwellings, as is commonly the case throughout the Mimbres Valley. While there is not enough of the walls above ground to show the former extent

---

[1] On some of the skulls excavated at Sikyatki, Arizona, in 1895, the author found concave disks of kaolin perforated in the center. One of these disks is represented in Fig. 356, p. 729, 17th Ann. Rep. Bur. Amer. Ethnol. In an article on " Urn Burial in the United States " (Amer. Anthrop., vol. 6, No. 5), Mr. Clarence B. Moore, quoting his own observations and those of many others, records burials in which an inverted mortar, bowl, basket, or other object was placed over the skull of the dead, and shows the wide distribution of the custom.

of the dwellings, the indications are that they were extensive and have been broken down and washed away.

OLDTOWN RUIN

Near where the Mimbres leaves the hills and, after spreading out, is lost in the sand, there was formerly a " station," on the mail route, called Mimbres, but now known as Oldtown. Since the founding of Deming, the railroad center, the stage route has been abandoned and Mimbres (Oldtown) has so declined in population that nothing remains of this settlement except a ranch-house, a school-house, and a number of deserted adobe dwellings.

Oldtown lies on the border of what must formerly have been a lake and later became a morass or cienega, but is now a level plain lined on one side with trees and covered with grass, affording excellent pasturage. From this point the water of the Mimbres River is lost, and its bed is but a dry channel or arroyo which meanders through the plain, filled with water only part of the year. In the dry months the river sinks below the surface of the plain near Oldtown reappearing at times where the subsoil comes to the surface, and at last forms Palomas Lake in northern Mexico.

In June, when the author visited Oldtown, the dry bed of the Mimbres throughout its course could be readily traced by a line of green vegetation along the whole length of the plain from the Oldtown site to the Florida Mountains.[1]

The locality of emergence of the Mimbres from the hills or where its waters sink below the surface is characteristic. The place is surrounded by low hills forming on the south a precipitous cliff, eighty feet high, which the prehistoric inhabitants chose as a site of one of their villages; from the character and abundance of pottery found, there is every reason to suppose this was an important village.

The Oldtown ruin is one of the most extensive seen by the author during his reconnoissance in the Deming Valley, although not so large as some of those in the Upper Mimbres, or on Whiskey Creek, near Central. Although it is quite difficult to determine the details of the general plan, the outlines of former rectangular rooms are indicated by stone walls that may be fairly well traced. There seem to have been several clusters of rooms arranged in rows, separated by square or rectangular plazas, unconnected, often with circular depressions between them.

---

[1] A beautiful view of the valley can be obtained from the top of Black Mountain, above the small ruin at its base, that will be mentioned presently.

There is considerable evidence of " pottery hunting " by amateurs in the mounds of Oldtown, and it is said that several highly decorated food bowls adorned with zoic figures have been taken from the rooms.   It appears that the ancient inhabitants here, as elsewhere, practised house burial and that they deposited their dead in the contracted position, placing bowls over the crania (fig. 1).[1]

The author excavated several buried skeletons from a rectangular area situated about the middle of the Oldtown ruin, surrounded on three sides by walls.   The majority of the dead were accompanied

FIG. 1.—Urn burial. (Schematic.)

with shell beads and a few turquoise ornaments, and on one was found a number of shell tinklers made of the spires of seashells. One of the skeletons excavated by Mr. Osborn appeared to have been enclosed in a stone cist with a flat slab of stone covering the skull. The remains of a corner post supporting the building stood upright on this slab.[2] In another case a skull was found broken into fragments by the large stone that had covered it. Several skeletons had no bowls

---

[1] The drawings of pottery designs in this article were made by Mrs. M. W. Gill; the stone and other objects were drawn by Mr. R. Weber.

[2] A significant feature in the Mimbres form of " urn burial " is the invariable puncturing of the bowl inverted over the head. The ancient Peruvians in some instances appear to have "killed" their mortuary bowls, and life figures depicted on Peruvian pottery are sometimes arranged in pairs as in the Mimbres.

over the heads, an exceptional feature in Mimbres burials; and in some instances the bowl had been placed over the face. In the case of numerous infant interments the bowl covered the whole skeleton.

RUIN ON BYRON RANCH

This ruin lies not far from the present course of the Mimbres near the Little Florida Mountains. The place has long been known as an aboriginal village site and considered one of the most important in the valley. The remains of buildings cover a considerable area. They have a rudely quadrangular form, showing here and there depressions and lines of stones, evidently indicating foundations of rooms, slightly protruding from the ground. Although this ruin has been extensively dug over by those in search of relics, no systematic excavations seem to have been attempted. It is said that valuable specimens have been obtained here, and fragments of pottery, arrowheads, and broken stone implements are still picked up on the surface.

The important discovery of burial customs of the ancient Mimbreños was made by Mr. Duff at this ruin. He excavated below the floor of one of the rooms and found a human cranium on which was inverted a food bowl pierced in the middle, the first example of this custom noted in the Mimbres region.

RUIN NEAR DEMING

About seven miles northwest of Deming, in a field on the north side of the Southern Pacific Railroad, there is a small tract of land

Fig. 2.—Paint mortar. Diam. 2½".

showing aboriginal artifacts strewn over the surface, affording good evidence of prehistoric occupation. There are no house walls visible at this place, and only a few fragments of food bowls, but in the course of an hour's search several small mortars (fig. 2), paint grinders and other objects were procured at this place.[1]

---

[1] Although not placed in the proper locality on his map, this ruin seems to be one of the "pueblos" (Nos. 162-164) mentioned by Dr. Hough.

PREHISTORIC SITE NEAR BLACK MOUNTAIN

Walls and outlines of rooms indicated by rows of stones mark remains of a prehistoric settlement at the base of Black Mountain, eight or nine miles northwest from Deming. Here occur many fragments of pottery, broken metates, and manos, and other indications of occupation by man. On top of Black Mountain there are rude cairns or rings of stones apparently placed there by human hands.

The fragments of pottery taken from the ruin at the base of Black Mountain are very different from those from Oldtown and other typical Mimbres ruins. Its color on the outside is red, with a white interior surface decorated with black geometric designs, the border is flaring often with exceptional exterior decoration. These bowls have broken encircling lines—a feature yet to be found in other Mimbres pottery—and none of the few pieces yet obtained from the ruin near Black Mountain has animal pictures. The whole appearance of this pottery recalls old Gila ware and suggests an intrusion from without the Mimbres region, possibly from the north and west.

The circles of stones on the top of Black Mountain have many points of resemblance to similar structures on hilltops near Swarts' Ranch on the Upper Mimbres, described by Mr. Webster, as follows:[1]

The tops of nearly all the mountains of this valley, and particularly those here mapped, are occupied by hundreds of rock mounds, breastworks, pits, etc. The region shown in plate 3, and which represents an area about one mile in length and three-fourths mile in width, exhibits 240 of these structures. . . . . These rock mounds are composed of more or less rounded rocks gathered from the region, and generally weighing from four to eight pounds each; although many are smaller: and again others weigh from twenty-five to fifty pounds or more each. These structures are generally circular: although at times they are ovate, and again assume an oblong or linear marginal outline. They vary considerably in size, although usually being only from three to four feet in diameter: the linear ones being from six to eight feet or more in length. Some of the larger circular mounds assume a diameter of seven to eight feet. The height of these mounds varies considerably; but as a rule assume a height ranging from one to one and a half feet.

The distance apart of these structures is variable; being as a general thing from five to fifteen feet; but not infrequently they are only two to four feet apart: at other times, however, they may be observed to be from sixty to ninety feet or more distant from each other.

---

[1] Archæological and Ethnological Researches in Southwestern New Mexico, Part 2, Ruin, Ancient Work Shop, Rock Mounds, etc., at Swarts' Ranch. (The Archæological Bulletin, vol. 4, No. 1, p. 14, 1913.)

Mr. Webster discovered on a rocky ridge near Swarts' ruin, somewhat higher on the Mimbres than Brockman's Mill, seven similar earthen pits of much interest, which remind the author of subterranean or half-sunken dwellings. They are saucer-shaped or linear depressions, averaging about two feet in depth; when circular they are from five to fifteen feet in diameter the linear form in one instance being fifty feet long. Some of these have elevated margins, others with scarcely any marginal ridge. The western margin in one instance has a " wall of rounded stones."

There are similar saucer-shaped depressions near Brockman's Mills and elsewhere in the Mimbres, almost identical with " pit dwellings " found by Dr. Hough near Los Lentes. These saucer-like depressions, often supposed to have been the pits from which adobe was dug, were also places of burial, the dead being presumably interred under or on the floors; the original excavation being a dwelling that was afterwards used as a burial place for the dead. Their form suggests the circular kiva of the Pueblos and has been so interpreted by some persons.

RUINS ON THE MIMBRES RIVER FROM OLDTOWN TO BROCKMAN'S MILLS

On low terraces elevated somewhat above the banks of the river, between Oldtown and Brockman's Mills, there are several village sites, especially on the western side.[1] The most important of these is situated about four miles north of Oldtown. The ruin at the Allison Ranch, situated at the Point of Rocks where the cliffs come down to the river banks, is large and there are many pictographs nearby. The ruins at Brockman's Mills on the opposite or eastern side of the river lie near the ranch-house. Many rooms, some of which seem to have walls well plastered, can be seen just behind the corral. North of the ruin is a hill with low lines of walls like trincheras. On some of the stones composing these walls and on neighboring scattered boulders, there are well-made pictographs.[2]

PICTOGRAPHS

Pictographs occur at several localities along the Mimbres. As these have a general likeness to each other and differ from those of other regions, they are supposed to be characteristic of the prehistoric

[1] For a description of ruins at Swarts' and Brockman's Mills see C. L. Webster, Archæological and Ethnological Researches in Southwestern New Mexico. (The Archæological Bulletin, vol. 3, No. 4.)

[2] It is said that a Spanish bell in the Chamber of Commerce at Deming, was dug up on this ranch near the ruin. This bell might indicate an old mission at this place.

FIG. 3.—Pictographs.

people. They are generally pecked on the sides of boulders or on the face of the cliffs in the neighborhood of prehistoric sites of dwellings. Although there is only a remote likeness between these pictographs and figures on pottery, several animal forms are common to the two.

The most important group of pictographs (fig. 3) seen by the author are situated about nine miles from Deming in the western foot-hills of Cook's Peak.[1] Some of the pictographs recall decorations on bowls from Pajarito Park.

Another large collection of Mimbres pictographs, visited by the author, is found at Rock Canyon, three or four miles above Oldtown, at a point where the cliffs approach the western bank of the river. On the river terrace not far above this collection of pictures, also on the right bank of the river, lies the extensive ruin of a prehistoric settlement, the walls of which project slightly above the surface. This ruin has been dug into at several points revealing several fine pieces of pottery, fragments of metates, and other implements, which are said to have been found in the rooms. A mile down the valley overlooking the river there is another cluster of pictures at a ruin called " Indian graveyard," probably because human skeletons have been dug out of the floors of rooms.

MORTARS IN ROCK IN PLACE

One of the characteristic features of the Mimbres ruins, but not peculiar to them, are mortars or circular depressions worn in the horizontal surface of rock in place. They are commonly supposed to have been used as mortars for pounding corn, and vary in size from two inches to a foot in diameter, being generally a foot deep. We find them occurring alone or in clusters. Good examples of such depressions are found near the Byron ruin, in the neighborhood of the ruins along Whiskey Creek, at Oldtown, and elsewhere. There is a fine cluster of these mortars nine miles from Deming, near the pictographs in the Cook's Range. Similar mortars have been repeatedly described and often figured. Mr. Webster has given the most complete account of this type of mortars in a description of the ancient ruins near Cook's Peak.[2] On the surface of the southwestern

---

[1] The author visited these rocks in company with Dr. Swope, who has known of them for many years.

[2] Archæological and Ethnological Researches in Southwestern New Mexico, Part 4. (The Archæological Bulletin, vol. 5, No. 2, p. 21.)

point of a low hill to the north of an ancient ruin at Cook's Peak, according to this observer,

occurs a feature which the writer had nowhere else seen, save on the east side of the same mountain. I refer to the great number of mortars which occur in this sandstone back a few feet to the north of the ruins, and which were made and long used by the ancient pueblo-dwellers. There exists at this one place fifty-three of these mortars, nearly all of them occurring in an area of surface not more than seventy-five or eighty feet in diameter. . . . . Nearly all the mortars are circular or sub-circular in outline, symmetrical and smooth inside, and the upper edge or margin usually rounded by the pestle. In a few cases, however, these mortars have an oblong or subovate outline, somewhat like some forms of metates found among the ruins.

These mortars often contract to a point at the bottom, when circular in marginal outline, although at times are longer than broad, as just stated, and in this case have a more flattened bottom. They vary from two to eleven inches in diameter, the smallest forms being those apparently only just begun, and are few in number. The deepest mortar observed was seventeen inches, though the great majority of them would vary perhaps from four to ten inches in depth. Often the rock was smooth and polished around the margin of the mortars, and [their distances apart] vary from a few inches to several feet from each other.

At times these mortars would be located on the top of a large block of sandstone which might happen to occupy this area; these boulders sometimes being four to five feet in diameter and perhaps four feet in height. It was plain to be seen that this ancient mill-site was long used by these peculiar people, but just why so many quite similar mortars should have been made here and used by these people is a matter of conjecture.

It seems certain that a sufficiently large number of people could not have been congregated here, under ordinary conditions, to warrant the forming of so many mortars for the purpose of grinding food.[1]

The present writer accepts the theory that these rock depressions were used in pounding corn or other seeds, but their great number in localities where ruins are insignificant or wanting is suggestive. We constantly find arable land near them, indicating that communal grinding may have been practised, and suggesting a large population living in their immediate neighborhood, which may have left no other sign of their presence.

MINOR ANTIQUITIES

The artifacts picked up on the surface near ruins or excavated from village sites resemble so closely those from other regions of the Southwest that taken alone these do not necessarily indicate special

---

[1] Mr. Webster describes "ancient pueblos" on the western side of this group of mountains as well as on the eastern slope of Cook's Range. Certain cave lodges, or walled caves, in a wild canyon on the east side of Cook's Peak are supposed by him to be the recent work of Apaches.

culture areas. A few of the more common forms from the Mimbres are here figured for comparison, but, with the exception of the pottery, there is little individuality shown in the majority of these objects. Among other objects may be mentioned stone implements, mortars, idols, bone implements, shell ornaments, and pottery.

STONE IMPLEMENTS

The stone axes are not very different from those of the Rio Grande and the Gila, but it is to be noticed that they are not so numerous as in

FIG. 4.—Stone axe.
Length 8¾".

FIG. 5.—Arrow polisher. Length 3¼",
breadth 2½".

the latter region, and are probably inferior in workmanship, fine specimens indeed being rare. The majority of the axes ·(fig. 4) are single grooved, but a few have two grooves. In Dr. Swope's collection, now in the Deming High School, there is a fairly good double-bladed axe.

Miss Alnutt, of Deming, has a remarkable collection of arrow-points gathered from many localities in the valley, and also a few fine spearpoints, conical pipes, and other objects taken from the sacred spring at Faywood Hot Spring. A beautiful arrow polisher found near Deming is shown in figure 5.

The pipes from the Mimbres take the form of tubular cloud-blowers, specimens of which are shown in figure 6. Apparently these pipes were sometimes thrown into sacred springs, but others have been picked up on the surface of village sites or a few feet below the surface.

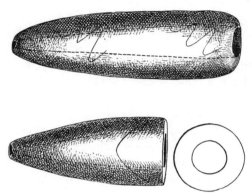

Fig. 6.—Cloud blowers. Faywood Hot Springs. (Swope collection.)
½ nat. size.

Lateral and top views of one of the characteristic forms of small stone mortars with a handled projection on one side is shown in figure 7. This specimen is in the Swope collection in the Deming

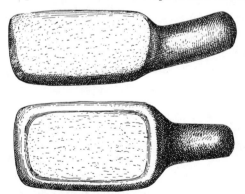

Fig. 7.—Handled mortar. (Swope collection.) Length 10¾".

High School. In the same collection there are also two beautiful tubular pipes, or cloud-blowers, from the same spring.

The stone mortars from Mimbres ruins vary in size. Many are simply spherical stones with a depression on one side; others are larger but still spherical, or ovate; while others have square or rectangular forms. The most remarkable feature in these is the presence of a handle on one side, which occasionally is duplicated, and in one instance four knobs or legs project from the periphery. These projections appear to characterize the mortars of the Mimbres, although they are not confined to them, as the form occurs in other regions of New Mexico and in California. One of the most instructive of these small spherical paint mortars, now owned by Mr. E. D. Osborn, has ridges cut in high relief on the outside.

Metates and manos, some broken, others whole, are numerous and can be picked up on almost every prehistoric site. While some of these metates are deeply worn, showing long usage, others have margins but slightly raised above the surface. The majority of metates found on the sites of habitations have no legs, but a typical Mexican metate with three knobs in the form of legs was presented to the National Museum by the Rev. E. S. Morgan, of Deming. Metates are sometimes found in graves with skeletons, presumably those of women. Several ancient metates are now in use as household implements in Mexican dwellings.

If the size of the population were to be gauged by the number of mortars and manos found, certainly the abundance of these implements would show that many people once inhabited the plain through which flows the Mimbres River. Narrow, flat stone slabs have an incised margin on one end. Their use is problematical. The frequency of stone balls suggests games, but these may have been used as weapons; or again, they were possibly used in foot races, as by the Hopi of to-day.

COPPER OBJECTS

Native metallic copper was formerly abundant at the Santa Rita mines, and there is every probability that the material out of which some of the aboriginal copper bells were made was found here, and that these mines were the source of float copper found in Arizona ruins. Although no copper implements were found by the author in the Mimbres ruins, he has been told that objects of copper apparently made by the aborigines have been found in some of the graves.[1]

---

[1] Elaborate metal objects of early historical times have been found at various places in the Mimbres. The best of these is a fragment of an elaborately decorated stirrup, now owned by Mr. Pryor of the Nan Ranch. A copper church bell was found near his house, and other metal objects belonging to the historic epoch are reported from various ruins in the valley.

STONE IDOLS

The author saw several stone idols that were reported to have been obtained from ruins in the Mimbres Valley. These idols represent frogs (fig. 8), bears, mountain lions, and other quadrupeds, and have much the same form as those from ancient ruins in Arizona.[1]

FIG. 8.—Frog fetish. Black Mountain Ruin. (Swope collection.) Length 3½".

On the backs of several of these stone idols are incised figures, like arrowheads tied to Zuñi fetishes, or possibly rain-cloud figures. In one instance they were made on an elevated ridge, which unfortunately was broken. The author has also seen several small amulets,

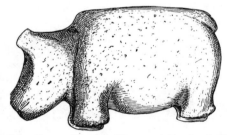

FIG. 9.—Fetish. Byron Ranch. (Swope collection.) Length 5¾".

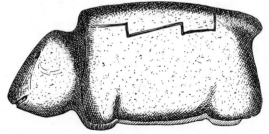

FIG. 10.—Fetish. Byron Ranch. (Swope collection.) Length 6¾".

perforated apparently for suspension. The stone idols here figured (figs. 8, 9, 10) were presented to the Deming High School by Dr. Swope.

---

[1] Similar stone idols from the San Pedro Valley and other localities, in Arizona and New Mexico, have mortar-like depressions on their backs.

SHELL BRACELETS AND CARVED SHELLS

Two or three shell bracelets were excavated from Mimbres ruins, and there were also found carved shells and tinklers not unlike those of northern New Mexico ruins. Some of these when excavated were found near the head and are supposed to have been earrings. Five shell rings were still on the bones of the forearm of a child when found. One of the shell bracelets owned by Mr. Osborn was cracked but was pierced on each side of the break, indicating where it had been mended; another had figures incised on its surface, and a third had the edges notched, imparting to it a zigzag shape, like that of a serpent. Many shell beads, spires of shells used for tinklers, and other shell objects, all made of genera peculiar to the Pacific Ocean, were found during the excavations.

POTTERY

FORMS AND COLORS

The comparatively large number of vases, food bowls, and other forms of decorated smooth ware in collections from the Mimbres is

Fig. 11.—Braided handle.
½ nat. size.

Fig. 12.—Small bowl.
Diam. 3½".

largely due to their use in mortuary customs, and the fact that almost without exception they were found placed over the skulls of the dead. Although the largest number of vessels are food bowls, there are also cups with twisted handles (fig. 11), bowls (fig. 12), vases, dippers, and other ceramic forms found in pueblo ruins.[1]

Coarse, undecorated vessels showing coils, indentations, superficial protuberances, and other rude decorations like those so well known in Southwestern ruins, are well represented. Some of these were

---

[1] One of the exceptional forms of pottery has a flat rectangular base, the four sides being formed by bending up segments of a circular disk (fig. 18).

used as cooking vessels, as shown by the soot still adhering to their outer surface. While the majority of bowls were broken in fragments when found, a few were simply pierced through the bottom; one or two were unbroken or simply notched at the edge.

The colors of Mimbres ware are uniform and often striking. There are good specimens of black and white ware; also red, black, and yellow with brown decorations are numerous. Some of the best pieces are colored a light orange. Many of the fragments are made of the finest paste identical in color and finish with ware from Casas Grandes, Chihuahua, which furnishes the best prehistoric pottery from the Southwest. No effigy jar, or animal formed vase, however, exists in any collections from the Mimbres examined by the author.

Ruins in the Lower Mimbres have thus far yielded a larger variety and a finer type of pottery than ruins on the banks of the river among the hills, which is in part due to the extent of excavations. The Old-town potters developed a kind of pottery with characteristic ornamentation found both in ruins in the plain to the south and along the narrow valley of the Mimbres to the north.

The Mimbres pottery, like all other ancient ware from the Southwest, frequently shows evidences of having been mended. Holes were drilled near the breaks and fibers formerly united the parts thus holding the bowl together even though broken. As one goes south, following the course of the river, the character of the pottery changes very slightly, but if anything is a little better.

The food bowls generally have a rounded base, but one specimen is flat on the bottom. The edges of the bowls from the ruin at Black Mountain are curved outward, an exceptional feature in ancient Pueblo vessels but common in modern forms.

PICTURES ON MIMBRES POTTERY

The great value of the ceramic collection obtained from the Mimbres is the large number of figures representing men, animals, and characteristic geometrical designs, often highly conventionalized, depicted on their interiors. These figures sometimes cover a greater part of the inner surface, are often duplicated, and are commonly surrounded by geometrical designs or simple lines parallel with the outer rim of the vessel. It is important to notice the graceful way in which geometrical figures with which the ancient potters decorated their bowls are made to grade into the bodies of animals, as when animal figures become highly conventionalized into geometrical designs. Although these decorations are, as a rule, inferior to those of the Hopi ruin, Sikyatki, the figures of animals are more numerous, varied, and realistic.

The ancients represented on their food bowls men engaged in various occupations, such as hunting or ceremonial dances, and in that way have bequeathed to us a knowledge of their dress, their way of arranging their hair, weapons, and other objects adopted on such occasions. They have figured many animals accompanied by conventional figures which have an intimate relation to their cults and their social organization. Although limited in amount and imperfect in its teaching this material is most instructive.

Fig. 13.—Hunters. Oldtown Ruin. (Osborn collection.)

GROUP OF HUNTERS

An instructive group of human figures is drawn on a deep red and white food bowl (fig. 13), which measures ten inches in diameter. It is evident that this design represents three hunters following the trail of a horned animal, probably a deer. This trail is represented on the surface of the bowl by a row of triangles, while the footprints of the hunters extend along its side. It may be noted that although there are three hunters, the trails of two only are represented, and that the hunters are barefoot. They have perhaps lost the trail and are looking the opposite way, while the animal has turned back on his path. The footprints of the deer in advance of the hunters are tortuous, showing want of decision on the part of the animal. The three hunters are dressed alike, wearing the close-fitting jacket probably made of strips of skin woven together like that found by Dr. Hough in a sacrificial cave at the head of the Tulerosa, New Mexico. Each carries a bow and arrow in his right hand, and in his left a stick which the leader uses as a cane ; the second hunter holds it by one end before him, and the third raises it aloft. These objects are supposed to represent either weapons or certain problematic wooden staffs with feathers attached, like divining rods, by which the hunters are in a magical way directed in their search. The first hunter " feels " for the lost trail by means of this rod.

An examination of the pictures of the arrows these hunters carry shows that each has a triangular appendage at the end representing feathers, and small objects, also feathers, tied to its very extremity. The hair of the third hunter appears to be a single coil hanging down the back, but in the other two it is tied in a cue at the back of the head. The eyes are drawn like the eyes on Egyptian paintings, that is, the eye as it appears in a front view is shown on the side of the head. The right shoulders of all are thrown out of position, in this feature recalling primitive perspective. The information conveyed by this prehistoric picture conforms with what is known from historical sources that the Mimbres Valley formerly abounded in antelopes, and we have here a representation of an aboriginal hunt.

FIGURE OF A WOMAN

A black and white bowl (pl. 1, fig. 1) is twelve and one-half inches in diameter and six inches deep. Upon this bowl is drawn a figure of a human being, probably a woman or a girl, seen from the front. Although portions of the figure are not very legible, such details as can be made out show a person wearing a blanket that extends almost to the knees leaving arms and legs bare, the lower limbs being covered. The head is square, as if masked, with hair tied at each lower corner. Although these appendages may be meant to represent ear-pendants, it is more likely that they are whorls of hair, as is still customary in Pueblo ceremonies in personations of certain maidens. Across the forehead are alternating black and white square figures arranged in two series, recalling corn or rain-cloud symbols. The neck is adorned by several strands of necklaces, the outermost of which, almost effaced, suggests rectangular ornaments. The garment worn by the figure is evidently the ceremonial [1] blanket of a Pueblo woman, for no man wears this kind of garment. It has a white border and from its middle there hangs a number of parallel lines representing cords or a fringe, evidently the ends of a sash by which the blanket was formerly tied about the waist. It is instructive to notice that we find similar parallel lines represented in a picture of a girl from Sikyatki [2] where the blanket has the same rectangular form as in the prehistoric Mimbres picture. There can be no question that in this case it represents a garment bound with a girdle, or that the picture was intended for that of a girl or a woman. We have in this picture evidence that the same method of arranging the hair was used in the Mimbres Valley as in northern New Mexico. The leg wrappings suggest those used by Pueblo women, especially the Hopi, whose leggings are made of long strips of buckskin attached to the moccasins and wound around the lower limbs.

PRIEST SMOKING

The third human figure, found on a black and white bowl from a Mimbres ruin, is duplicated by another of the same general character depicted on the opposite side of the bowl. These figures (fig. 14) are evidently naked men with bands of white across the faces. The eyes are represented in the Egyptian fashion. In one hand each figure holds a tube, evidently a cloud-blower or a pipe, with feathers attached to one extremity, and in the other hand each carries a triangular object resembling a Hopi rattle or tinkler. The posture of these figures suggest sitting or squatting, but the objects in the extended left hand would indicate dancing. The figure is identified as a man performing a ceremonial smoke which accompanies ceremonial rites.

MAN WITH CURVED STICK

One of the most instructive food bowls found at Oldtown, now owned by Mr. Osborn, has on it a picture of two hunters, one on each side of an animal (fig. 15). One of these hunters carries in his hand a stick crooked at the end, its form suggesting a throwing stick.[3] Both hunters have laid aside their quivers, bows, and arrows, which are shown behind them. The picture of an animal between them has been so mutilated by " killing " or breaking the bowl that it is impos-

---

[1] Called also a " wedding blanket " since it is presented to a girl on marriage by her husband's family.

[2] 17th Ann. Rep. Bur. Amer. Ethnol., pl. 129, fig. *a*.

[3] The hand of the hunter pictured on a bowl already described (fig. 13), also carried a curved stick.

Fig. 14.—Priest smoking. Osborn Ruin.

Fig. 15.—Man with curved stick. Oldtown Ruin. (Osborn collection.)
Diam. 5½".

sible to identify it. From the end of this crook to the body of the animal there extend two parallel lines of dots indicating the pathway of a discharged weapon. Near the body of the animal these rows of dots take a new direction, as if the weapon had bounded away or changed its course. The rows of dots are supposed to represent lines of meal by which Pueblos are accustomed to symbolically indicate trails or " roads."

There is, of course, some doubt as to the correct identification of the crooked staff as a throwing stick, for as yet no throwing stick has been found in the Mimbres ruins. The resemblance of the crooked stick to those on certain Hopi altars and its resemblance to emblems of weapons carried by warrior societies is noteworthy. Crooked sticks of this character have been found in caves in the region north of the Mimbres.[1]

We find a survival of a similar crook used as sacred paraphernalia in several of the Hopi ceremonies, where they play an important rôle. As the author has pointed out, crooked sticks or gnelas (fig. 16) identified as ancient weapons surround the sand picture of the Antelope altar in the Snake Dance at Walpi, and in Snake altars of other Hopi pueblos, but it is in the Winter Solstice Ceremony, or the Soya-luña, at the East Mesa of the Hopi, that we find special prominence given to this warrior emblem. During this elaborate festival every Walpi and Sitcomovi kiva regards one of these gnelas as especially efficacious for the warriors, and it is installed in a prominent place on the kiva floor, as indicated in the author's account of that ceremony.[2]

The following explanation of these crooks was given him by the priests:

These crooks or gnelas have been called warrior prayer sticks, and are symbols of ancient weapons. In many folk tales it is stated that warriors overcame their foes by the use of gnelas which would indicate that they had something to do with ancient war implements. Their association with arrows on the Antelope altars adds weight to this conclusion.

The picture from Oldtown ruin of the hunter who has laid aside the quiver, bow, and arrow, and is using a similar gnela,[3] corroborates this interpretation.

Not all crooked sticks used by the Hopi are prayer sticks, or weapons, for sometimes in Hopi ceremonials a number of small shells are

[1] Bull. 87, U. S. National Museum.
[2] The Winter Solstice Ceremony at Walpi. Amer. Anthrop., 1st ser., vol. 11, Nos. 3, 4, pp. 65-87, 101-115.
[3] An ancient crook found in a cave near Silver City is figured by Dr. Hough. Bull. 87, U. S. National Museum.

tied to the extremity of a crooked stick forming a kind of rattle. In the Flute Ceremony a crooked stick is said to be used to draw down the clouds when the rain they contain is much desired.

Figure 16 is a representation of one of the crooks which was specially made for use in the Soyaluña at Walpi, in 1900. Similar crooks were set upright in a low mound of sand on the floors of all the kivas. Extending from the base of the crook to the ladder there

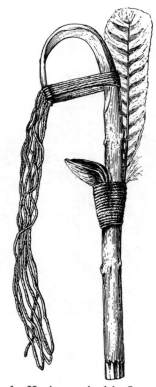

FIG. 16.—Hopi curved stick. Length 8″.

was sprinkled a line of meal called the road (of blessings), over which was stretched a feathered string attached to the end of the crook. Midway in the length of the crook was attached a packet of prayer meal wrapped in cornhusk and a feather of the hawk, a bird dear to warriors, and other objects, which indicated a prayer offering. At the termination of ceremonies in which these crooks are made and blessed as prayer emblems by the Hopi they are deposited in shrines as recorded.

The crook (gnela) is used as a prayer emblem of warriors because it has the form of an ancient weapon, and while it assumes modifications in different Hopi ceremonies it apparently has one and the same intent, as in Soyaluña. This crook is sometimes interpreted as symbolically representing an old man with head bent over by age, but this interpretation is probably secondary to that suggested above, as so often happens in the interpretations given by primitive priests.

The true interpretation of the crooked prayer stick was pointed out by the author in his article on " Minor Hopi Festivals," [1] as follows:

This crook is believed by the author to be a diminutive representation of an implement akin to a throwing stick, the object of which is to increase the

FIG. 17.—Human figure running. Oldtown Ruin. (Osborn collection.)
Diam. 7½".

velocity of a shaft thrown in the air. Its prototype is repeatedly used in Hopi rites, and it occurs among Hopi paraphernalia always apparently with the same or nearly the same meaning.

In figure 17 is represented a person running with outstretched banded arms, holding in the left hand a bow, and in the other a straight stick. The head is circular with cross lines, a round, dotted eye, and two triangular ears. Another representation shows a human figure with a bow and arrow before the hands, accompanied by three animals, the middle one being a bird and the two lateral, quadrupeds.

[1] Amer. Anthrop., n. s., vol. 4, p. 502.

By far the most unusual group of human forms consists of two figures, one male, the other female, depicted on another bowl. The action in which these two are engaged is evident. The female figure has dependent breasts and wears a girdle. One hand is raised and brought to the face and the other carries a triangular object. The female figure has three parallel marks on the cheek, like the Hopi war-god. Behind the woman are several curved lines depicting unidentified objects.

The figure shown on one bowl (fig. 18) has several marked features, but the author is unable to suggest any theory of identification. It seems to be a seated figure with a human head, arms, and legs, the toes and fingers being like hands and feet. The forearm is drawn on the shoulder in the same way as in the one of the hunters (fig. 13).

FIG. 18.—Unidentified animal and bowl of unusual form. Oldtown Ruin. (Osborn collection.)

The eye, nose, and mouth are also human, but the body is more like that of an animal. The appendages back of the head are similar to those interpreted as feathers on the heads of certain animal designs.

On the theory that this is a seated human figure it is interesting to speculate on the meaning of the curved object represented on the surface of the bowl, extending from one hand to the foot. This object has the general form of a rabbit stick or boomerang, still used by the Hopi in rabbit hunting.[1]

---

[1] Rabbits are abundant in the Mimbres Valley and several well-drawn pictures of this animal are found on the pottery.

The well-drawn figure painted on a bowl (pl. 1, fig. 2) from Oldtown ruin represents a man with knees extended and arms raised as if dancing. This picture has characteristic markings on the face, but otherwise is not distinctive.

QUADRUPEDS

Wolf.—Although there are not sufficiently characteristic features represented in the next figure (pl. 2, fig. 1) [1] to identify it satisfactorily, the form of the head, tail, mouth, and ears suggests a wolf.[2] The square design [3] covering one side of the body seems to the

Fig. 19.—Antelope. (Osborn collection.) Diam. 10".

author not to belong to the animal itself, for an Indian who could represent an animal as faithfully as those here pictured would not place on it such markings unless for a purpose. It resembles the small blankets sometimes worn by pet dogs or horses among white people, which is a lame explanation, as dog and horse blankets were

---

[1] This picture resembles that of a wolf depicted on the east wall of the warrior chamber at Walpi. See Amer. Anthrop. n. s., vol. 4, pl. 22.

[2] Pictures of the mountain lion by Pueblo artists, at least among the Hopi, have the tail turned over the back. The animal on the Mimbres bowl having no horns is not a horned deer or antelope.

[3] The decoration of the bodies of animals with rectangular figures is a common feature in Mimbres pottery, as will be seen in pictures of birds soon to be considered.

unknown among Indians. The only theory the author has formed regarding this geometrical figure is that it is a variant of the Sikyatki habit of accompanying a figure of an animal with a representation of his shrine. This bowl is of black and white ware and is eleven inches in diameter by five and one-half inches deep.

Antelope.—There are two[1] figures of an animal with branching horns,[2] supposed to be an antelope, an animal formerly common in Mimbres Valley. In one of these (fig. 19) the head is held downward as if the animal were feeding; in the other (fig. 20) the neck is

FIG. 20.—Antelope. Osborn Ruin. Diam. 10″.

extended. A pair of markings on the neck are identical with those on pictures of the antelope still painted on modern pottery made by the Zuñi. A band, resembling a checkerboard, is drawn across the body of one; on the other are parallel lines.

Another figure referred to as an antelope appears to represent a young fawn, since, while it has all the characteristics of this animal,

[1] In addition to the figure with the hunters which is probably a deer, as it has not the antelope marks on the neck.

[2] These horns are represented on a plane at right angles to that in which they naturally lie.

the horns are wanting. This specimen (fig. 21) was found at Oldtown. The rectangular shape so often given to the bodies of animals
drawn on Mimbres pottery is well shown in this specimen.

FIG. 21.—Fawn. Oldtown Ruin.

FIG. 22.—Rabbit. Oldtown Ruin. Diam. 7½".

Mountain Sheep.—It is evident from the form of the unbranched
horns, the slender legs, and the head, that either a mountain sheep or
mountain goat was intended to be represented in plate 2, figure 2.

The markings on the body are symbolic, suggesting lightning, and it may be added that the Hopi depict the lightning on the artificial horns mounted on caps and worn by them in presentations of dances in which they personate mountain sheep.

Rabbit or Hare.—The pictured representation (fig. 31) of a quadruped whose hindlegs are larger than the forelegs and whose long backward extending ears are prominent features, probably represents a rabbit or a hare. The eyes recall figures of birds depicted on bowls from the Little Colorado ruins in Arizona, where eyes are

Fig. 23.—Mountain lion or wild cat.   Fig. 25.—Bird E. Osborn Ruin.
     (Osborn collection.)   (Osborn collection.)

depicted on one side of the head in violation of a law of perspective in which only one eye can appear on a lateral view. The figure appears to have a tuft of grass in the mouth. The geometric markings on the body are different from those of any known species of rabbit and belong to the category of symbolic designs.

The author excavated at Oldtown a food bowl, the figure on which was undoubtedly intended for a rabbit (fig. 22). The head, ears, body, legs, and tail are well made, leaving no question of the intention of the artist; but if there were any doubt of the identification it is dispelled by the representation of the mouth, on which the sensitive hairs or bristles are represented.

Mountain Lion.—One of the Oldtown bowls is decorated with a representation of the wild cat or mountain lion, and is a fair example of archaic design (fig. 23). The feature that distinguished this quadruped is the position of the tail which, like those of Pueblo pictures of mountain lions or cats, is bent forward over the back.

Both head and body are rectangular and the legs are short and stumpy with sharp curved claws. The ears, mouth, and teeth have characteristic features of carnivora and the tail is banded, especially near the end.

The geometric design on the side of the body consists of an angular, S-shaped design with two equal armed stars, the latter associated with the mountain lion in Pueblo symbolism. The single figure drawn on this bowl occupied the middle of the interior, but in the next bowl this figure is duplicated.

The two figures on another bowl also represent some cat, or mountain lion, but the geometric figure on its body differs so much from the first specimen that it may belong to a different genus. The geometrical designs occur on both the anterior and posterior extremities of the rectangular body and consist of triangular figures with parallel lines and terraces recalling rain-clouds. This bowl is owned by Mr. E. D. Osborn, and was found at Oldtown. The decorations on the two quadrants alternating with the animal figures are bands from which other markings radiate to the side of the bowl.

Badger.—The quadruped drawn on the inside of a bowl found at Oldtown, and now owned by Mr. E. D. Osborn, has some resemblances to a badger, especially in the head, ears, teeth, and tail. The geometrical design on the body of this animal consists of an unequal sided rectangle enclosing four triangles with angles so approximated as to form an enclosed rectangle. The head has two bands extending longitudinally, apparently conventionalized markings characteristic of this animal, as they do not occur on deer, wildcats, or mountain sheep.

Birds.—As has been pointed out in the author's identifications [1] of designs on Sikyatki pottery, those representing birds are among the most abundant. The same holds also in the pottery from the Mimbres, where several figures identified as birds occur on food bowls. Two of these are duplicated on the same vessel, practically the same figure being repeated on opposite sides. In the latter case each member of the pair faces in an opposite direction or is represented as if moving with the middle of the bowl on the left. [2]

---

[1] 17th Ann. Rep. Bur. Amer. Ethnol., p. 682.

[2] This is known as the sinistral circuit and is regarded as beneficial in Hopi ceremonials.

The various birds differ considerably in their forms, organs, attitudes, and appendages. Two of the pictures seem to represent the same bird, but the others belong to different genera. There are one or two figures in which feathers can be distinguished, but as a rule they are fewer in number and the feathers less conventionalized than in Sikyatki pottery.

Pending the difficulty in identifying the various designs representing birds, they are designated by letters A, B, C, D, etc.

Bird A.—The figure shown in plate 3, figure 1, is represented by two designs, practically the same, repeated so far as appendages go, but quite different in the ornamentation of their bodies. One of these has the same geometrical figure on its body as on one of the quadruped pictures, the second has a different design. Both birds have wings outspread as if in flight, in which the feathers are well drawn in detail, especially the wing on the side turned toward the observer. That on the opposite side is simply uniformly black. The feathers of its companion on the other side of the bowl are indicated by parallel lines. The tail is long and forked at the extremity, suggesting a hawk, and is decorated for two-thirds of its length with cross-hatched and parallel lines. A triangular appendage arises from the under side of the tail at the point where the line decoration ends, forming an appendage which is likewise represented in the companion picture.

Bird B.—Bird B (pl. 3, fig. 2) is painted on the interior of a food bowl of black and white ware, ten inches in diameter by five inches deep. Its body is oval, the head erect and undecorated, and the tail twisted from a horizontal into a vertical plane as is customary in representation of lateral views of birds from Pueblo ruins. The geometric figure on the body is unfortunately somewhat obscured by the plaster used in mending, but several parallel bars that may represent feathers of the wings show through it, and a number of other designs or parallel lines are apparent. An appendage of triangular form hangs from the lower margin of the body and indicates the position of one leg; the other leg is missing.

Bird C.—Bird C, shown in plate 4, figure 1, occurs on a black and white bowl that measures ten inches in diameter, five and one-half inches in depth. The figure occupies the circular zone in the middle of the bowl and is enclosed by parallel lines which surround the bowl near the rim. The top of the head, which is globular, is white in color, the beak projecting and the eyes comparatively large. The body is likewise globular and is covered by a square geometrical design the details of which are considerably obscured by the hole in the middle of the jar. A number of parallel lines of unequal length, turned downward, hang from the rear of the body and form the tail. The long legs suggest a wading bird, and the widely extended claws point to the same identification.

Bird D.—One of the most instructive figures of birds occurs on a bowl from Oldtown ruin. This bowl (fig. 24) is now owned by Mr. E. D. Osborn, by whom it was found. The bird depicted on it is seen from the back; its wings are drooping, and parallel lines indicate feathers. The legs, drawn backward, terminate in three toes, and the tail, slightly bent to one side, is composed of several feathers.

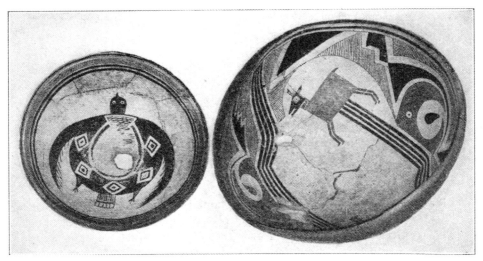

FIG. 24.—Bird D.   FIG. 29.—Unidentified animal. Oldtown Ruin.
(Osborn collection.)   (Osborn collection.)

The head is globular with two eyes on the back and a short pointed beak. As in all other zoic figures the geometric figures on the back of the body are the most characteristic. The middle of the body is occupied by an oval design through which may be seen the perforation with which the bowl was killed. At one end there is a triangular design with cross lines which extend partly over the oval figure where, except at one point, they are obscure.

Four quadrilateral designs are distributed at intervals around the oval figure. Each of these has sides of about equal length and a dot medially placed in a smaller figure contained in a larger.

Bird E.—The bird shown in figure 25 (p. 35) from the Osborn ruin has a body form not unlike that of plate 4, figure 1, but the geometric design on the body, although rectangular, has incurved sides and is covered with cross lines suggesting a net. Its neck is girt by four rings, head small, without feathers, eye minute, bill comparatively long and pointed recalling that of a snipe which is also suggested by long legs and in a measure by the form of the tail.

This bird is undoubtedly aquatic, as indicated by the figure of a fish which it appears to be on the point of capturing or devouring.

Bird F.—The bird shown in plate 4, figure 2, is different from any of the above and is distinguished readily by the four curved lines on. the head suggesting the quail. The pointed tail is marked above and below with dentations, formed by a series of rectangular figures which

FIG. 26.—Bird G. Oldtown Ruin. (Osborn collection.) Diam. 10″.

diminish in size from body attachment to tip. The body itself is marked posteriorly with parallel lines, rectangular and curved figures suggesting wings.

The bowl (fig. 26) has three animals figured upon it forming a graceful combination. The most striking represents a long-billed bird with one wing notched on the inner margin. The tail of this bird is differently drawn from any of the other birds in the collection and has representations of six feathers. In front of this bird, with the point of the snout at the tip of the bill of the bird, is a lizard-shaped head covered with scales and two round eyes. The other remarkable figure also has extended forelegs, but the body is so broken that identification is quite impossible. Like the figure of the lizard, it also has a lozenge head and two eyes. The geometrical designs on the body are characteristic.

ANIMALS NOT IDENTIFIED

Unidentified Animal.—It is difficult to tell exactly what animal was intended to be represented by that shown in plate 5, figure 2. Its head and mouth are not those of any of the horned animals already considered, although it has some anatomical features recalling a mountain sheep. The extension back of the body has a remote likeness to a fish, but may be a bird or simply a conventional design. The geometrical figure covering the side of the body bears some likeness to one depicted on a bird, as shown in plate 3, figure 1. The same geometrical figure sometimes also occurs separated from any animal form in Sikyatki pottery.[1]

The bowl is ten inches in diameter, five inches in depth, and the figures are painted red on a white ground.

Unidentified Animal.—One of the most remarkable of many figures on bowls from Oldtown in the collection of Mr. E. D. Osborn is shown in figures 27, 29 (p. 38). Three colors enter into the decoration of this bowl, black, white, and brown, and there are two types of ornamentation, one zoic, the other geometric. The bowl itself was much broken when found, but not so mutilated as to hide the main designs.

The zoic figures represent animals with square bodies, four legs, ears, head, and tail like a young antelope. There is no design on the side of the body, but in its place four broad parallel bands extend from the belly across the bowl. Each group of parallel lines changes its direction, widening in their course or near the ends where they enlarge for the accompanying figure. The markings on the necks of these figures suggest those on fawns.

The elaborate geometric figure composed of a scroll and comma-like dot and eye is a highly conventionalized symbol, possibly of some animal, as a bird's head, common on Casas Grandes pottery.

There is a bowl on exhibition in the Chamber of Commerce at Deming with a picture of a quadruped resembling a deer, but the base is so fractured in killing that it is difficult to determine the shape of the body or its decoration.

Unidentified Animal.—One of the most instructive figures of the collection appears in duplicate on a large food bowl (pl. 5, fig. 1). This vessel is black and white in color and measures fifteen inches in

---

[1] 17th Ann. Rep. Bur. Amer. Ethnol., pls. 121*a*, 138*c*. There are one or two examples of Sikyatki pottery where a geometrical design is attached to an animal figure which leads to the belief that possibly the figure attached to the rear of the above may not represent a part of another animal but rather a geometrical design of unknown significance, in this particular recalling old time Hopi ware.

diameter by six inches deep. The two designs occur on the two sides of the interior of the bowl, the middle of which is left without decoration.

The body of this creature is elongated and tapers backward, being continued into a tail like that of the lizard. The head is long and the snout pointed. Only two legs are represented, and these are situated far back on the body near the point of the origin of the tail from the body. A lozenge-shaped symbol forms the geometrical design on the side.

Fig. 27.—Unidentified animal. Oldtown Ruin. (Osborn collection.)

The presence of only two legs in this figure would seem to indicate that a bird was intended, but no bird has a tail like this figure; and the prehistoric potters of the Mimbres certainly knew how to draw a bird much better than this would imply. The exceptional features of this drawing, doubtless intentional, belong neither to flesh, fish, nor fowl, rendering its identification doubtful.

GRASSHOPPER [1]

A figure on a bowl here represented (pl. 6, fig. 1) is painted in "black or brown on a background of bluish wash over a yellow color."

[1] This figure may also be identified as a locust.

This bowl is eleven inches in diameter, five inches in depth. The figure is a remarkable one, having features of several animals, but none of these are more pronounced than its insectiform characters, among which may be mentioned the antennæ, three legs on one side (evidently three pairs of legs, for that in the back is simply introduced in violation of perspective), and an extended segmented abdomen attached to the thorax and terminating in a recurved tip. The character of the appendages to the thorax, or the wings, leaves no doubt that a flying animal was intended, and the legs and head being like an orthopterous insect, it may be provisionally identified as a " grasshopper." [1]

While the general form of head, thorax, and body appear from an inspection of the figure, it may be well to call attention to certain special features that illustrate primitive methods of drawing. The most striking of these is seen in the abnormal position of the leg which arises from the thorax on the back in the rear of the so-called wings. This abnormal position was introduced by the artist to show the existence and form of the legs on the right side; the appendage corresponds with one of the three on the left side, which have the proper position but are much smaller. A similar delineation of organs out of place not seen or turned away from the observer was common among the prehistoric artists of the Pueblo region and is paralleled by the representation of two eyes on one side of the head already mentioned. The two " wings," each ending in white circles with dots or crosses, are supposed, on the theory that this is a grasshopper, to represent wing covers or elytra, which of course the prehistoric people of the Mimbres did not differentiate from folded wings. It is possible that wing cover and wing may be represented on one side and that corresponding organs on the right side of the body are omitted. The thorax is covered with regularly arranged rows of dots formed by parallel lines crossing at an angle, forming purely arbitrary decoration representing the geometric designs on the bodies of other animals.

FROGS AND BIRDS

One of the few bowls obtained on which animals of two species were depicted on the same vessel was excavated by the author at Oldtown. This remarkably fine specimen (pl. 7, fig. 1) has figures of

---

[1] Possibly depicted on a food bowl because grasshoppers were eaten by the prehistoric people of the Mimbres.

two birds and two frogs [1] drawn in opposite quadrants, being unique in this particular. The two birds and frogs are not very unlike those already described but have certain characteristic features, especially in the geometric designs on their bodies.

The bowl is warped into an irregular shape and made of thin ware, probably distorted in firing. It was found under the floor of one of the central rooms in the Oldtown ruin, almost completely covering the skeleton of a baby.

On another bowl (pl. 6, fig. 2) there is depicted a frog very like that last mentioned. The frog being an amphibian was undoubtedly greatly reverenced by the ancient people of the Mimbres Valley.

HORNED SNAKE

The serpent with a horn on the head is pretty generally regarded as a supernatural being, and its pictures and effigies occur on modern Hopi, Zuñi, and other Pueblo paraphernalia. It is an ancient conception, for it is figured on prehistoric pottery from all parts of the Pueblo area, having been found as far south as Casas Grandes in Chihuahua. It is to be expected that a people like the ancient Mimbreños who adorned their pottery with so many well drawn zoic figures would have included the horned serpent, provided this reptile was a member of their pantheon. The nearest approach to a figure of such a monster is found on a large pottery fragment found by Mr. Osborn twelve miles south of Deming. This fragment covered the cranium of a skeleton and was perforated or " killed " like a whole bowl.

A very large number of pictures of the horned snake from localities all over the Southwest might be mentioned, but a few examples are adequate to show how widespread the conception was in ancient times. They occur among the Tewa, Keres, Zuñi, Hopi and other Pueblos and vary greatly in details, but in all instances preserve the essential symbolic feature—a horn on the head and a serpentine body.

The horned serpent is known to the Hopi as the plumed serpent, and when represented by them has a bundle of hawk feathers as well as a horn attached to the head. Effigies of this being, also with horn

---

[1] A picture of a horned toad on a food bowl was recorded from Cook's Peak by Professor Webster, and there is a picture of what appears to be the same reptile in Mr. Osborn's collection. It is of course sometimes difficult to positively distinguish representations of frogs, toads, lizards, and Gila mon-sters, but the anatomical features are often well indicated.

and feathers, are used in several ceremonies, as the Winter Solstice,[1] and a dramatic festival[2] which occurs yearly in March. Wooden representations of the same horned snake are carried as insignia by a warrior society called the Kwakwantu,[3] in the New Fire Ceremony. The priests of the Tewan pueblo, Hano, among the Hopi also have effigies of the horned snake, the worship of which their ancestors brought to Arizona from New Mexico. These effigies are yearly made of clay and form conspicuous objects on the December altars of that pueblo.

FIG. 28.—Serpent. Osborn Ruin. (Osborn collection. E. D. O. Jr. del.)

The head shown in figure 28 has a horn curving forward almost identical with that on the head of a horned serpent on a bowl from Casas Grandes in the Heye collection. Its gracefully sinuous body is decorated with alternating geometric figures, curves and

---

[1] The Winter Solstice Ceremony. Amer. Anthrop., 1st ser., vol. 11, Nos. 3, 4, pp. 65-87, 101-115.

[2] A Theatrical Performance at Walpi. Proc. Washington Acad. Sci., vol. 2, pp. 605-629. Native pictures of the Hopi horned snake may be found, pl. 26, 21st Ann. Rep. Bur. Amer. Ethnol.

[3] The horned serpent cult at Walpi is said to have been introduced from the south.

straight lines.[1] Accompanying the figure of a serpent is a well-drawn picture of a turtle which is decorated on the carapace with a rectangular area on which is painted a geometric figure recalling that on bodies of birds and some other animals.

FISHES

One of the bowls (fig. 30) from the Oldtown ruin has two fishes depicted on opposite sides of the inner surface. These fishes resemble trout and are of different colors, black and reddish brown figures

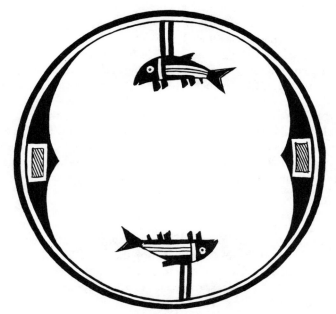

Fig. 30.—Fish. Oldtown Ruin. Diam. 9".

painted on a white ground. . They are represented as hanging from two parallel lines surrounding the rim of the bowl. These fishes are so well drawn that there is no doubt what animal was intended to be here represented. On the interior of another bowl excavated by the author at Oldtown there is a picture of a fish which recalls the two

---

[1] Of all the designs representing the horned snake known to the author this picture from the Mimbres resembles most closely the pictures of this being on pottery from Casas Grandes. It has, however, the single horn found on the clay image in the Hano altar of the Winter Solstice Ceremony, although quite unlike figures on pottery from the Pajarito region. The bodily decorations in the Mimbres bowl are unlike those of the Hopi horned snake.

just mentioned.[1] It may be mentioned that fishes are not represented in the beautiful specimens of pottery from Sikyatki,[2] possibly for the simple reason that there are no streams containing fish in the neighborhood of Hopi ruins. In the Mimbres, however, fish are still found and were no doubt formerly abundant and well known to the prehistoric inhabitants,[3] being looked upon by them as water symbols in much the same way as the frog is at present regarded by Zuñi and Hopi.

Another fish figured on a bowl from Oldtown, is unfortunately broken near the tail. The accompanying decoration has apparently another figure behind this fish, but its complete form is obscured by the perforation made in killing the vessel.

The most problematical of all the life figures on the Mimbres pottery is shown in plate 7, figure 2. This figure occurs on a black and white food bowl, eleven inches in diameter, four and one-half inches in depth. In support of the theory that the two figures here depicted represent fishes, we have the pointed head without neck, the operculum as a white crescentic design, two fins (pectoral. ventral, ·and anal), the median (adipose?) dorsal fin unpaired, and a long tail bifurcated at the extremity. The resemblance of these figures to the undoubted fishes on bowls previously mentioned is conclusive evidence that they represent the same animal.

GEOMETRICAL FIGURES

The geometrical designs on Mimbres pottery are rectangular, curved, and spiral, the first form being the most common. These units are arranged in twos or fours, and although they consist often of zigzag or stepped figures, the triangle and rectangle predominate. The geometrical designs are rarely colored, but commonly filled in with hachures and parallel lines. There are seldom decorations on the outside of the Mimbres bowls, in which respect they differ from ancient Hopi (Sikyatki) vessels elsewhere figured.[4] Conversely, that part of the interior of the bowl which surrounds the central design, oftentimes elaborately ornamented in Mimbres pottery, is very simply

---

[1] The Mimbres formerly had many more fishes than at present, and Bartlett records that his men often brought in fine trout for his camp. These, with turkeys, quail, deer and antelopes, led him to say that his " fare might be called sumptuous in some respects " (op. cit., p. 236).

[2] Fishes are sometimes represented on Keresan pottery.

[3] As elsewhere mentioned in this paper, one of the bird figures (fig. 25) has a fish in its mouth.

[4] 17th Ann. Rep. Bur. Amer. Ethnol., Part 2, figs. 277-355.

decorated in Sikyatki pottery. Encircling lines on Mimbres pottery are continuous, whereas at Sikyatki they are broken at one or more points by intervals known as the " life gateways " or " lines of life." [1] The geometrical figures on the inside of every bowl sometimes surround a central region on which no figures of animals or human beings are drawn, but which is perforated.

The more strikingly characteristic forms of geometrical figures are shown in designs on plate 8. Certain of the geometrical figures drawn on the sides of animals as on the wolf (pl. 2, fig. 1), the antelope (figs. 19 and 20), the mountain sheep (pl. 2, fig. 2), the unidentified animal and bird (figs. 18 and 25), the reptile (fig. 28),

Fig. 31.—Rabbit and geometrical designs.

also appear without the animals and probably have the same significance [2] in both instances.

No geometrical figures were identified as representing sun, moon, earth, or rain-clouds. A few crosses, circles, triangles, and irregular quadrilateral designs combined with zigzag stepped figures and interlocked spirals and highly interesting swastikas (fig. 31) form the

---

[1] Ceremonially, every piece of pottery is supposed by the Hopi to be a living being, and when placed in the grave of the owner, it was broken or killed to let the spirit escape to join the spirit of the dead in its future home. There is no evidence that the Sikyatki mortuary pottery was purposely broken when deposited in the grave, and probably no need of perforating it to allow free exit of the spirit, for the broken encircling line, "life gateway," absent in Mimbres pottery, but almost universally present in ancient Hopi pottery, answered the same purpose, in their conception.

[2] Following Hopi analogies, where these geometrical figures frequently occur with animals they may have the same symbolic meaning as when alone, and represent shrines or prayer-offering houses.

4

majority of the designs.[1] Several geometric designs, as those on the
bodies of figures 25 and 26, appear on Sikyatki pottery (see 17th Ann.
Rep. Bur. Amer. Ethnol., plate 121) ; others resemble Pueblo symbols
of wide distribution, but the majority are unique. The geometric
designs on the bodies of life-figures vary with the animal depicted,
but the same genus of animals does not always have the geometric
figure, although almost identical designs occur on the bodies of
different genera. It is recognized that a comparison of designs on
Southwestern pottery shows a general uniformity in geometrical pattern which renders it very difficult to distinguish different local areas
of development, and may be the result of more extensive inter-

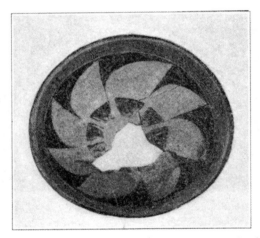

FIG. 32.—Geometrical figure. (Osborn collection.)

change of ideas and a greater uniformity of cultural conditions. The
pottery of the Mimbres shares with the rest of the Southwest several
well-known geometrical designs which no doubt date back to an
earlier epoch than the evolution of animal figures, but it also has several decorations of geometrical patterns (fig. 32) that are peculiar to
it and which, taken with the characteristic zoic figures, serve to differentiate it from other local areas. Mimbres pottery as pointed out by
others has a general likeness to that from Casas Grandes Valley in
Chihuahua, a resemblance which no doubt increases as we follow the
river to Lakes Palomas and Guzman.[2] The resemblance is not close

---

[1] Unfortunately there are few decorated vases represented in the collection,
but exploration in the field may later bring many of these to light.

[2] The author brought to Washington fragments of a food bowl from the ruin
near Byron Ranch, identical with Casas Grandes ware.

enough to indicate identity, but we have enough material to support the belief that the archeological area in which it occurs is Mexican, unlike that of any other ceramic area in Arizona or New Mexico. Here a specialized symbolism has been developed which is different from that of the Rio Grande, or the Upper Gila-Salt area, and that characteristic of the great Lower Gila in which lie the compounds like Casa Grande. The Mimbres Valley archeologically is the northern extension of a culture area which reached its highest development on Casas Grandes River.

Conclusions

Geographically the Mimbres Valley is the northern extension of the drainage area of the large interior plateau, the lowest level of which is occupied by Palomas, Guzman, and other so-called lakes. The Casas Grandes, Mimbres, and other rivers contribute their scanty waters to these lakes, which have no outlets into the sea. As a rule the thirsty sands along the course of the river drink up the surplus waters of the Mimbres or cause them to sink beneath the surface, to reappear when the configuration of lower clay or rock formations forces them from subterranean courses. Considering the similarity in climatic and geographical conditions in the northern and southern ends of this plateau, we would expect to find cultural likenesses in the prehistoric inhabitants of the Mimbres and Casas Grandes valleys, but such is not the case. The absence of relief decoration combined with painting, so common in the pottery from the Casas Grandes region, separates the Mimbres ware from that found far to the south.[1]

There are evidences that the course of the Mimbres River through Antelope Plain has from time to time changed considerably, and although a section of its bed now lies east of the Florida Mountains, the river probably formerly made its way to the west of the same in its course to Mexico. Modifications or changes in the bed of this river have had in the past much to do with the shifting of population and obliteration of prehistoric sites, either by washing them away entirely or burying them out of sight or deeply below the surface. This concealment of evidences of prehistoric occupancy has also been aided by frequent sandstorms, when considerable quantities of soil have been transported from place to place and deposited on walls or covered implements lying on the surface of the ground. It is also

---

[1] We must look to renewed explorations to shed light on this and many other questions which the paucity of material is yet insufficient to answer.

possible that there has been a slow change of climate, causing a desic-
cation which may have been so widespread that the inhabitants of the
plain were driven up river into the hills where water was more
abundant, but it is well to remember that abandoned settlements or
ruins exist on the banks of the Mimbres where there is still abundant
water, as well as in the plain which is dry.

The depth of the present water level, as shown by drilling for wells,
varies in different places in the valley, but in the neighborhood of the
hills there are many springs. The configuration of the surface of the
hard clay strata lying beneath the soil here and there often forces the
water to rise to the surface, and ruins occur at points where at present there are no signs of surface water, although at the time they
were inhabited there may have been more water.[1] Whether or not
this water was brought to certain ruins by a system of artificial irri-
gation, the canals of which have been obliterated, we cannot say, but
there is only scanty evidence that the climate here, as elsewhere, has
radically changed since man occupied the valley.[2]

Although there is a remote likeness between the terraced house or
pueblo community of northern New Mexico[3] and the prehistoric
houses of the Lower Mimbres, its closest resemblance is to an ante-
cedent type, for it is possible that the terraced pueblo culture in the
Rio Grande Valley was preceded by another. This earlier type of
habitation of the Mimbres Valley was like the fragile-walled house of
the natives inhabiting a large part of Arizona and New Mexico
before the Puebloan, and we have evidence that this older style of
building was scattered over the present Pueblo area. There is no
evidence of a terraced dwelling or pueblo more than one story high

[1] In dry seasons the river flows under the superficial soil at a varying depth,
but in floods it follows the surface bed.

[2] As the author has pointed out in several articles, the abandonment of
Southwestern ruins is due to a variety of causes, chief of which are changes
of climate. It is often due to other more local causes, as attacks by hostiles,
salinity of soil, poor site for defence, presence of wizards, contagious dis-
eases, etc.

[3] The designation "pueblo ruins" sometimes applied to any cluster of ancient house walls in Colorado, Utah, New Mexico, and Arizona, should be
restricted to a well-defined architectural type which originated and reached
its highest development in a small area in New Mexico. It was eventually
carried by colonists in all directions from the center of origin, becoming in-
trusive as far west as the Hopi, Zuñi, and Little Colorado. The boundaries
of this type never extended into Mexico in prehistoric times. The ruins along
the Mimbres are not community houses of terraced character and should not
be called pueblo ruins.

in the Mimbres or the inland basin in which it lies. In other words the ruins of the Mimbres may be regarded as older than true pueblo ruins, resembling an earlier type of dwelling that antedated, in the Rio Grande Valley, the terraced houses.

The author does not find any architectural features in the remains of the prehistoric habitations of the Mimbres Valley suggesting Casa Grande compounds, or those massive buildings with encircling walls which are characteristic of the plains of the Gila. Although the walls of the Casas Grandes, in Chihuahua, are constructed in the same way and out of material like those of Casa Grande on the Gila, the architectural feature, an encircling wall of the latter, has not yet been recognized on the Sierra Madre plateau.[1] Objects found in the Gila ruins are somewhat different in form from those of Chihuahua, while pottery from the Gila Valley ruins and that from the inland plateau in northern Chihuahua is markedly different, with very divergent symbolism. Not only do forms of stone implements of a shape unknown in southern Arizona occur in southern New Mexico, but also the methods of disposal of the dead differed among the two people. The latter practised inhumation only, the other both cremation and inhumation. The aborigines of the Mimbres Valley placed a bowl over the head or face of the dead, a practice which, so far as known, does not appear to have been so commonly in vogue in inhumation of the prehistoric people of the Lower Gila plains.

The conventional geometric symbols on prehistoric Mimbres pottery are readily distinguished from those on ware from Tulerosa, a tributary of the San Francisco. The most significant feature of the Mimbres pottery is that fifty per cent of the figures on it represent men or animals, while out of a hundred bowls from the Gila not more than two or three are ornamented with zoic designs. As we know comparatively nothing of the pottery of the sources of the Upper Gila and that part of its course which lies between the Tulerosa and the Mimbres, we can at present venture very little information on ceramic relations, but similarities or mixtures would naturally be expected, due to contact or overlapping, the type of the one valley overlaying that of the other or mingling with it.

The sources of the Upper Salt, the largest tributary of the Gila, lie far from the Mimbres, and close relationship in the pottery of the

---

[1] This statement is made with reservation, as the true architectural form of the Casas Grandes of Chihuahua is not yet known. The published plans show no encircling wall like that of Casa Grande on the Gila; probably the Casas Grandes of Chihuahua belong to a highly specialized type different from others.

ancient people inhabiting its banks is not found or expected. It is not known whether the pottery from the Upper Salt and that from the Upper Gila is similar, for our museums have no extensive collections from the latter region from which to make comparisons and draw conclusions. We know practically nothing of the prehistoric culture of the Upper Gila.

The aborigines of the Mimbres, like those of some of the former dwellers in Pajarito Park in New Mexico, practised a modified form of urn burial, but the latter rarely decorated their pottery with figures of animals. As compared with known Pueblo ceramics, the Mimbres pottery appears to be more closely allied to ancient Keresan than to old Tewan. Judging from what remains, the houses architecturally had little in common with true pueblos.[1] There are no evidences of circular subterranean kivas with pilasters, ventilators, deflectors, and niches, as in northern New Mexico, although there is a fairly large proportion of subterranean rooms or pit dwellings which may have been their prototypes. Architecturally the prehistoric habitations of the Mimbres Valley represent an old house form widely distributed in the Pueblo region or that antedating the pueblo or terraced-house type before the kiva had developed.

There are not sufficient data at hand to determine satisfactorily the kinship of the prehistoric inhabitants of Mimbres Valley, but as far as may be judged by pottery symbols it may be supposed that their culture resembled that of other sedentary people of New Mexico and Arizona in early times, as well as that of peoples of Chihuahua. It appears to the author that there are so many cultural similarities among the sedentary people which inhabited the Sierra Madre plateau, of which the Antelope Plain of Mimbres Valley is only a northern extension, that we may regard their culture as closely related. A specialized high development of this inland culture took place along the Casas Grandes River, culminating in Chihuahua. The Mimbres Valley was inhabited by people somewhat less developed in culture.

Although the ancients of the Mimbres were related on the one side to the Pueblos of New Mexico and on the other to more southern people, that relationship existed between the ancestors of the same rather than with modern Pueblos, and reached back to a time before

---

[1] While neither the terraced nor the "compound" type of architecture has been seen in the Mimbres for the reason that both were specialized in their distinct geographical areas, the fragile-walled, jacal type of habitation is identical in form, though not in time, in all three localities.

the terraced communal house type originated. This type of house arose in northern New Mexico and spreading from this center extended down the San Juan as far as the Hopi, while modifications are also found in certain ruins on the Gila and Little Colorado, which, like Zuñi, it profoundly influenced, but its influence never reached as far as the Lower Mimbres.

A comparison of the limited archeological material from the Mimbres with that from other localities in the Southwest suggests a provisional hypothesis that the prehistoric culture of this valley was not modified by terraced architecture nor greatly affected by that of the Lower Gila type, both of which evolved independently and locally, but belonged to an older type with which it had much in common.

1

2

FIG. 1.—WOMAN DANCER. BLACK AND WHITE WARE. 12 BY 6 INCHES. OSBORN RUIN
FIG. 2.—DANCING FIGURE. RED DECORATION. DIAMETER 5 INCHES. OSBORN RUIN

FIG. 1.   TWO WOLVES.   BLACK AND WHITE WARE.   11 BY 5½ INCHES.   OSBORN RUIN

FIG. 2.   MOUNTAIN SHEEP.   BLACK AND WHITE WARE.   11 BY 5½ INCHES.   OSBORN RUIN

1

2

FIG. 1.—BIRD A. RED AND WHITE WARE. 9 BY 4 INCHES. OSBORN RUIN
FIG. 2.—BIRD B. BLACK AND WHITE WARE. 10 BY 5 INCHES. OSBORN RUIN

FIG. 1. BIRD C. BLACK AND WHITE WARE. 10 BY 5½ INCHES. OSBORN RUIN

FIG. 2. BIRD F. RED AND WHITE WARE. DIAMETER 8 INCHES. OSBORN RUIN

1

2

FIG. 1.—PROBLEMATICAL ANIMAL. BLACK AND WHITE WARE. 15 BY 6 INCHES. OSBORN RUIN

FIG. 2.—PROBLEMATICAL ANIMAL. RED DECORATION. OSBORN RUIN

VOL. 63, NO. 10, PL. 6

FIG. 1.—GRASSHOPPER. RED FIGURE. DIAMETER 5 INCHES. OSBORN RUIN
FIG. 2.—FROG. DIAMETER 10 INCHES. OSBORN RUIN

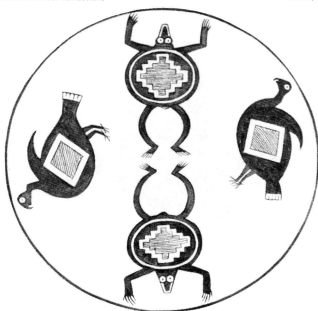

FIG 1.   FROGS AND BIRDS.   BLACK AND WHITE WARE.   DIAMETER ABOUT 12 INCHES
OLDTOWN RUIN

FIG. 2.   FISHES.   BLACK AND WHITE WARE.   11 BY 4½ INCHES

GEOMETRICAL DESIGNS.   DIAMETER 1/7 NATURAL SIZE

DESIGNS ON PREHISTORIC POTTERY
FROM THE MIMBRES VALLEY,
NEW MEXICO

Avanyu Publishing Inc.

SMITHSONIAN MISCELLANEOUS COLLECTIONS

VOLUME 74, NUMBER 6

DESIGNS ON PREHISTORIC POTTERY FROM THE MIMBRES VALLEY, NEW MEXICO

BY

J. WALTER FEWKES

Chief, Bureau of American Ethnology

(PUBLICATION 2713)

CITY OF WASHINGTON

PUBLISHED BY THE SMITHSONIAN INSTITUTION

MAY 29, 1923

DESIGNS ON PREHISTORIC POTTERY FROM THE MIMBRES VALLEY, NEW MEXICO

By J. WALTER FEWKES

CHIEF, BUREAU OF AMERICAN ETHNOLOGY

Before the year 1914 little was known of the manners and customs of the prehistoric inhabitants of the valley of the Rio Mimbres in southern New Mexico. Historical references to these people from the time this valley was discovered to its occupation by the United States are few and afford us scanty information on this subject. Evidence now available indicates that the prehistoric occupants had been replaced by a mixed race, the Mimbreños Apache, of somewhat different mode of life. Until a few years ago the numerous archeological indications of a prehistoric population were equally limited. Some of the earlier writers stated that there are no evidences of a prehistoric sedentary population occupying the area between Deming, New Mexico, and the Mexican border.

In his pamphlet on the " Archeology of the Lower Mimbres Valley, New Mexico," published in 1914,[1] the author reviewed the contributions of others on this subject up to that date, and the present paper offers, as a supplement to that preliminary account, descriptions of additional designs on pottery collected by several persons since the publication of the article above mentioned. The writer has laid special stress on the quality of realistic designs on pottery from this region, and has urged the gathering of additional information on their meaning and relationship.

In the author's judgment no Southwestern pottery, ancient or modern, surpasses that of the Mimbres, and its naturalistic figures are unexcelled in any pottery from prehistoric North America. This superiority lies in figures of men and animals, but it is also *facile princeps* in geometric designs. Since the author's discovery of the

---

[1] Smithsonian Misc. Coll., Vol. 63, No. 10. Supplementary additions were made in the " Explorations and Field-Work of the Smithsonian Institution in 1914," pp. 62-72, Smithsonian Misc. Coll., Vol. 65, No. 6, 1915; and in the American Anthropologist, n. s. Vol. XVIII, pp. 535-545, 1916.

main features of this pottery the Mimbres Valley has come to be recognized as a special ceramic area.

Specimens of this pottery were first called to the attention of the author in 1913 by Mr. H. D. Osborn, of Deming, New Mexico, who excavated a considerable collection of this ware[1] from a village site near his ranch 12 miles south of Deming. Shortly after the discovery the author visited the location where it was found and excavated a small collection. From time to time since the author first announced the discovery of this material, years ago, other specimens of the same type have been described by him. These objects support early conclusions as to the high character and special value of this material in studies of realistic decoration. New designs have been added to available pictographic material which justify these conclusions.

In the past year (1921) Mr. Osborn has continued his excavations and obtained additional painted bowls, thereby enlarging still more our knowledge of the nature of the culture that flourished in the Mimbres before the coming of the whites. These newly discovered specimens are considered in the following pages.[2]

A brief reference to a physical feature of the Mimbres Valley may serve as a background for a study of the culture that once flourished there. The isolation of this valley is exceptional in the Southwest. The site where the Mimbres culture developed is a plateau extending north and south from New Mexico over the border into Mexico. Ranges of mountains on the east side separate it from the drainage of the Gulf of Mexico and high mountains prevent the exit of its rivers on the west. Its drainage does not empty directly into the sea, but after collecting in lakes it sinks into the sands. The lowest point of this isolated plain in which are the so-called lakes, or " sinks," Palomas and Guzman, is just south of the Mexican line. The water of the Mimbres sometimes finds its way into the former, but is generally lost in the sands before it reaches that point. The Casas

---

[1] Many of these specimens were purchased by the Bureau of American Ethnology and are now in the U. S. National Museum, but the majority were later sold to Mr. George G. Heye and are now in the Museum of the American Indian, New York.

[2] Several other collectors have furnished me with data on Mimbres ware, among whom Mrs. Edith Latta Watson, and Mrs. Hulbert, of Pinos Altos, New Mexico, should be especially mentioned. On the very threshold of his descriptions the author desires to thank Mr. Osborn, Mrs. Hulbert and Mrs. Watson for permission to describe this new material. He desires also to commend the beautiful copies of photographs of the designs on these bowls, made by the artist, Mrs. George Mullett, of. Capitol View, Maryland.

Grandes and tributary streams that lie in the basin south of the national boundary flow northward and finally empty into Lake Guzman. It is characteristic of the upper courses of these streams that they contain abundant water, while lower down they sometimes sink below the surface, but still continue their courses underground unless rock, clay or other formations that the water can not readily penetrate have pushed up their beds to the surface.

Flowing water is constant in the upper Mimbres but lower down the valley it is subterranean, though rising at times to the surface. The river is indicated here and there by rows of trees or a series of ponds. Water is never found in great abundance, but there is always enough for trout and a few other fishes which the early inhabitants, judging from the number of these animals depicted on pottery, admired and greatly esteemed for food.

There is more water in the Casas Grandes River and its tributaries than in the Mimbres, which is smaller and has fewer branches. There is a remarkable natural hot spring in the Mimbres Valley at Faywood, in which a large number of aboriginal implements and other objects were found when this spring was cleaned out several years ago, leading to the belief that it was regarded by the aborigines as a sacred spring.

The forms of pottery found in the Mimbres Valley differ very little from those of the pueblo areas. Food bowls predominate in number, although effigy vases, jars, ladles, dippers, and similar objects are numerous in all collections from this locality. They belong to modified black and white ware, red on white, unglazed, generally two-colored types. There are also specimens of uncolored, corrugated and coiled ware.

As the author has elsewhere indicated,[1] the figures on Mimbres pottery are largely realistic. A reference to an early account of the fauna might be instructive as an indication of the motives of the decoration of this pottery.

" The hills and valleys," writes Bartlett,[2] " abound in wild animals and game of various kinds. The black-tail deer (*Cervus lewisii*) and the ordinary species (*Cervus virginianus*) are very common. On the plains below are antelopes. Bears are more numerous than in any region we have yet been in. The grizzly, black, and brown varieties are all found here ; and there was scarcely a day when bear-

[1] Archeology of the Lower Mimbres Valley, New Mexico, Smithsonian Misc. Coll., Vol. 63, No. 10, 1914.
[2] Personal Narrative, 1854.

meat was not served up at some of the messes. The grizzly and brown are the largest, some having been killed which weighed from seven to eight hundred pounds. Turkeys abound in this region, of a very large size. Quails, too, are found here; but they prefer the plains and valleys. While we remained, our men employed in herding the mules and cattle near the Mimbres often brought us fine trout of that stream, so that our fare might be called sumptuous in some respects."

The above mentioned animals and many others are represented on ancient Mimbres pottery. There are a few paintings of flowers but only rarely have natural objects such as sun, moon, mountains, or hills been identified. Of geometrical designs there are zigzags, terraces, circles, rectangles, spirals, and conventionalized heads, beaks, feathers and the like of birds; but food animals are the most abundant, deer, antelope, turkeys, rabbits and the like predominating. We have every reason to suppose from the pictography on the pottery that animal food formed a considerable part of the dietary of the ancient Mimbreños, but there is also abundant evidence that they were agriculturists and fishermen.

As a rule the bowls on which the designs here considered are depicted were mortuary, that is, found buried with the dead under the floors of former houses. These bowls are almost universally punctured or "killed" and are commonly found at the side of the skeleton, although when it is in a sitting posture, as often occurs, the bowl covers the head like a cap.

The Mimbres pottery shows several designs representing composite animals, or those where one half of the picture represents one genus of animal and the other a wholly different one. Similar composite pictures are rarely found in American art, although there are several examples of feathered and bicephalic serpents, winged reptiles, and the like. Probably if we were familiar with the folklore of the vanished race of the Mimbres we would be able to interpret these naturalistic pictures or explain their significance in Indian mythology.

The attention given to structural details in the figures of animals shows that the ancient inhabitants of the Mimbres who painted these designs were good observers, clever artists, and possibly drew these pictures from nature. There are, however, anomalies; profiles of the tails of birds are drawn vertically and not represented horizontally; the feathers that compose them were placed on a plane vertical, not horizontal, to the body. Both eyes were rarely placed on one side of the head as is so often the case with bird figures from the ancient pottery. They are often lozenge shape but generally round. Birds are the most common Mimbres animal paintings and the details of different kinds of feathers are often so carefully worked out that they can be distinguished. Many birds are represented as destitute of wings or have them replaced by geometrical figures of various angular shapes.

The designs here described support the theory already published, that the pottery of the Mimbres is related to that of Casas Grandes in Chihuahua, Mexico, but there are significant differences between the houses of the two areas. The Casas Grandes culture apparently extended northward into New Mexico and penetrated to the sources of the Mimbres River. In this uniquely isolated valley, whose rivers had no outlets in the sea, there developed in prehistoric times one of the most instructive culture areas of the Southwest. The geographical position renders it most important to investigate as it lies midway between the Pueblo and Mexican region, showing affinities with both.

The majority of designs on Casas Grandes pottery are drawn on curved surfaces, as terra cotta vases, jars, and effigies, while those on Mimbres ware are depicted on a flatter surface—the interior of food bowls. For this reason the spaces to be filled on the former are more varied; but the style in the two types is practically the same.

The designs of Mimbres ceramics are painted on the inside surface of clay bowls, the color of which is white, red, brown, or black. While the majority of the designs are depicted on the *inside* of Mimbres food bowls, similar geometric figures occur on the *outside* of Casas Grandes vases, dippers, ladles, cups, and other forms. A food bowl furnishes a plane inner surface but its rounded exterior is the least desirable for realistic figures. In these characters we have one of the important points separating the pottery of the Mimbres from that of Casas Grandes.

Effigy jars and vases, predominating in collections from Casas Grandes, are rare in those from near Deming and on the upper Mimbres. The pottery from at least one village site of the Mimbres resembles that of the upper Gila and its tributaries; but both shards and whole pieces of pottery from the Gila are characteristic and can readily be distinguished from that of the Mimbres-Casas Grandes region. The decoration of Mimbres pottery is distinctive and very different from that on any other prehistoric pueblo ware, evidently little modified by it. Although highly developed and specialized like modern pueblo pottery, it is quite unlike that from ancient pueblos of the Rio Grande region.

We find in this pottery well drawn naturalistic pictures as well as geometric designs, but there is no new evidence that the former were developed forms of the latter. It is more than probable that both geometric and realistic types were made contemporaneously and originated independently. By many students geometric ceramic decorations are supposed to be older than realistic; straight lines, dots, circles, stepped figures and spirals are supposed to precede life figures. Others hold that conventionalized designs follow naturalistic forms. It is sometimes supposed that in the growth of decorative art lines or dots are added to meaningless figures to make them more realistic. For instance, three dots were added to a circle to bring out a fancied human face, or representations of ears, nose, and other organs were annexed to a circle to make a head seem more realistic. Lines are thus believed to be continually added to a geometric meaningless figure to impart to it the life form.

There is a certain parallelism in these figures to drawings made by children to represent animals, whose pictures are often angular designs rather than realistic portrayals of objects with which they are familiar. It may be pointed out that some children in their earliest drawings make naturalistic, others geometric figures.

Naturally, when we contrast the designs on pottery from the Mimbres with that of the Mesa Verde, one great difference outside of the colors is the large number of realistic figures in the former and the paucity of the same or predominance of the geometric type in the latter. If we compare the designs of Sikyatki pottery with those on the Mimbres ware the differences are those of realism and conventionalism. The designs of Sikyatki pottery are mainly conventionalized animals, while those of the Mimbres are realistic. Geometrical designs from Mesa Verde are not conventionalized life forms; neither are they realistic. The pottery of the Little Colorado is midway in type, so far as its decoration goes, between that of Sikyatki and Mesa Verde. It is not as realistic as the Mimbres, not as conventionalized as Sikyatki, nor as geometric as Mesa Verde.

There seems much to support the theory that these three types of design, geometric, conventionalized, and realistic, are of equal age and developed independently. The author inclines to the belief that the primitive artist, having noticed certain resemblances in his geometric designs to life forms, men or animals, helped out the fancied likeness by adding dots or lines for eyes, nose and mouth, wings, legs or tail, to a circular or rectangular figure, and thus made a head of a man or an animal, the result being a crude realistic figure. Subsequent evolution was simply a perfecting of this figure. The theory that the conventional figure was derived from the realistic also appeals to the author; and he further believes that there are many geometric decorations that have no symbolic significance.

The naturalistic designs on pottery of the modern pueblos of Keresan stock resemble somewhat those of the Mimbres, or are closer to them than those of the modern Tewa, Zuñi, or Hopi; while, on the other hand, ancient Tewa, Zuñi, and Hopi wares are closer to Keresan than they are to modern pottery of the same pueblos. Ancient Hopi and Zuñi designs resemble each other more closely than modern, a likeness due in part to their common relationship to the culture of the Little Colorado settlements, the differences being due to the varying admixture of alien elements. In fact, the archaic pottery symbols are simpler than the composite or modern.

Human figures on Mimbres pottery are as a rule cruder than those of animals and in details much inferior to those of birds. They represent men performing ceremonies, playing games, or engaged in secular hunting scenes, and the like.[1] Now and then we find a representation of a masked man or woman in which the face is sometimes decorated with black streaks as if tattooed or painted. Frequently there are representations of feathers or flowers on body, limbs or head. Both full face and profiles of men occur in these figures; even the hair dressing is shown with fidelity. Several styles of clothing are recognizable. Let us now proceed to discuss a series of these figures.

HUMAN FIGURES

Figure I represents men engaged in a hunt. A hunter carries in his right hand three nooses attached to sticks; in his left he holds a stick to which feathers or leaves are attached. The hunter's hair is tied down his back; apparently he wears a blanket or loose fitting garment. Five groups of upright sticks support horizontal ones; that at the extreme right has attached to it a noose still set. Three captured birds are seen in the remaining nooses. The double row of dots represents a trail; two birds to the right of the human figure

---

[1] Why the figures on Mimbres pottery should be more realistic than those from elsewhere in the Southwest is not apparent, unless the richness of the fauna has some connection with it.

face three sticks. The whole picture represents a method of snaring birds that was in vogue among the Mimbres ancients.

Figure 2 is also instructive. It is evidently a gambling scene representing three men playing the cane dice game, widely distributed among our aborigines. Unfortunately almost a half of the picture is no longer visible, but three cane dice appropriately marked lie in the middle of what remains of a rectangular design on the bottom of a broken jar. As the game requires four cane dice, two are missing. On one side of the figure is what appears to be a basket of arrows, evidently the stakes for which the game is being played. One of the seated human figures holds a bow and three or four arrows, while another has only one arrow. Rows of dots extending across the bowl are visible under the feet of the figure with one arrow.

There are six human figures represented in figure 3, five of which in a row appear to be crawling up a ladder while a sixth, bearing in the left hand a crook, is seated in an enclosure near the end of the ladder. The attitude of the five climbing figures suggests men emerging from the earth; the chamber in which the sixth is seated resembles a ceremonial room or kiva.

In figure 4 we have three human figures, two seated and one lying down. The difference between these figures is not great, but the two seated figures have their hair tied in a knob; the hair of the horizontal figure is straight. The left-hand figure bears a zigzag object in his hand that reminds one of a snake or lightning symbol. The right-hand figure appears to hold in his hand an implement represented by parallel lines and dots surmounted by an imitation of a head with feathers. This object calls to mind the wooden framework used by the Hopi in their ceremonies to imitate the lightning.

In figure 5 there are four figures, all different; two were evidently intended to represent men with human bodies and heads of animals. Each carries a rattle in one hand and a stick to the end of which is attached a feather, or a twig with leaves, in the other.

The exact signification of the group of three figures, two male and one female, shown in figure 6, is not evident. The two men carry sticks with attached flowers, or figures of the sun or a star; the other figure, which represents a woman, has a crook in one hand. The frayed edge of the woven belt she wears hangs from her waist.

The knees of the two human figures shown in figure 7 rest on the back of a nondescript animal. The figures are evidently duplicates, the only difference being in the forms of the geometric figures depicted on the bodies of the animals.

Two nicely balanced human figures shown in figure 8 are represented as resting on a quadrilateral object decorated with zigzag markings, like symbols of lightning.

The heads in figure 9 are human but the body and limbs are more like those of quadrupeds.

The method of drawing the human figure in figure 10 is very characteristic. Here we evidently have a representation of a dancer, whose body is painted black, surrounded by a white border.

The human figures thus far considered are drawn in colors on a white background. Not so those that follow. In figure 11 there are two negative figures, representations of human beings placed diametrically opposite each other, and, similarly arranged, two turkeys painted black on a white oval area, a very good example of the arrangement of double units. The human figures are white and have arms and legs extended. A black band in which are two eyes extends across the forehead. The lips are black; mouth white. This is a good example of one pair of units being negative, the other positive. There are four triangles with hachure in the intervals between the figures.

An analysis of the design in figure 12 shows two human figures drawn opposite each other, with arms extended and legs similar to those of frogs. The complicated geometric figures vary considerably but can be reduced to about three units; but these units are not always repeated twice.

In figure 13 there are two human figures, one seated on the shoulders of the other, who is prostrated and has head severed from body. The former apparently is holding a knife or pipe in his right hand and the hair of the decapitated head in the left. The head and back of this seated figure is covered with what appears to be a helmet mask and animal's pelt. The mask resembles the head of a serpent or some reptilian monster that has a single apical horn on the head and jaws extended. Possibly the disguise represents the Horned Serpent or the same being as figure 41. The body of the man and the lower part of the face is black. The Snake priests at Walpi paint their chins black.

ANIMALS

Quadrupeds.—Many of the animals depicted on the bowls are mammals distinguished by four legs, but often these present strange anomalies in their structure. In several pictures of rabbits and some other quadrupeds the lower fore-legs bend forward, and in one instance, a composite animal, the fore-legs are short and stumpy with no indication of a joint, but the hind-legs are slender, longer than the fore-legs, and apparently belong to a different animal. The majority of all the mammals represented have geometric designs on the body.

Variations in the form of the head and mouth are noticeable and are important in the determination of different genera to which these mammals belong. Figure 14 represents two quadrupeds with heads of lions and two geometric designs irregularly terraced, with white border. The interior is marked with parallel lines. The head is short and calls to mind that of a carnivorous animal; there is a white band about the neck; the tip of the tail is white. The rectangular body marking is lozenge-shaped with dots.

Figure 15 represents an unknown quadruped resembling some carnivorous animal. The tail has a white tip like figure 14; the ears are more prominent and pointed.

In figure 16 two men are dragging an animal by ropes tied to the neck of the captured beast. This is an effective way of leading a dangerous animal and preventing it from attacking either one of them.

The head and fore-legs of figure 17 resemble those of the bison. The head has ears, a horn, and a cluster of five feathers that are grouped fan-shape. The rear end of the body and hind-legs are somewhat like those of a wolf. This is a mythological composite animal or two different animals united.

The animal shown in figure 18 is seated, and has tail and ears like those of a hare or rabbit. The head, however, resembles that of a human being, with two black marks on the white cheeks. The upper part of the head is black. The two marks on each cheek among the Hopi are symbols of the Little War God.

Two exceptional animals with tails flattened like beavers are represented in figure 19. Although the fore-legs bear claws the posterior legs are club-shaped or clavate. The distribution of white and black on the bodies indicates a partly negative and partly positive drawing. The mouth has the form of a snout.

It would seem that figure 20 represents a carnivorous animal like a mountain lion. The tail is coiled, ending in a triangular appendage. Head, ears, and claws like a cat. The checkerboard periphery design is particularly effective.

Figure 21 represents a rabbit or hare whose body is black and without ornament. The joints of the legs bend in an unnatural way. Ears, tail, and labial hairs recall a rabbit.

Figure 22 represents two negative pictures of rabbits with characteristic ears and tails. They are separated by a band composed of parallel lines, somewhat after the style of figure 9. Space between fore- and hind-legs is filled in with white zigzag lines. Two rabbits also appear in figure 23, the forms of ears, tail, and body being somewhat different.

Figure 24 is likewise a rabbit figure which resembles the preceding in color. Most figures of rabbits have black bodies without the decorations on other mammals.

The food bowl illustrated in figure 25 has thirteen clusters of feathers, each cluster composed of four feathers, making an ornamental periphery. These clusters are called feathers because of their resemblance to the feather in a bird's wing depicted in figure 54. Although the two figures have rabbit features, the feet are quite different from those of that animal, the legs ending in sickle-like appendages. The reason for the strange shape of the fore and hind feet of this picture is unknown.

The body of the quadruped shown in figure 26 appears to have been penetrated by four arrows, but the central portion of the bowl has been broken or " killed " and an identification of the figure is impossible. The neck is long, quite unlike that of any animal known in the Mimbres fauna.

The animal represented in figure 27 is probably a bat; in no other representation is a realistic zoic figure so closely related to the geometric design.

Figure 28 resembles a frog, and figure 28a suggests two tadpoles crossed over a disk on which are depicted eight small circles. The petal-like bodies radiating from the central disk are ten in number, four of which are primary, four double, and two single. A much better figure of a frog is shown in figure 29.

Reptiles.—Figures 30 and 31 have closer likenesses to turtles than to frogs. The resemblance to a turtle is very striking in figure 31. The tail, which is absent in pictures of frogs, is here well developed, and the eyes and legs differ from those of frogs. The carapace of figure 31 is covered with scales.

Figures of a serpent and a mountain sheep are shown in figure 32. The two animals in figure 33 appear to be lizards outlined in white on a black ground; a kind of negative picture in which the body is filled in with black.

The animal shown in figure 34 is apparently a lizard, but it differs from the other figures of lizards in the bifurcated head, lizards generally being represented with lozenge-shaped heads.

The two reptilian figures shown in figure 35 have all the characteristics of lizards and the picture probably illustrates some myth or folk-tale. The mouths of the two lizards and that of the bird are approximated, which would suggest that the three were talking together.

Fishes.—The representation of a fish (fig. 36) between two birds suggests the aquatic habits of the latter. The form of the fish suggests the garpike, but the tail is more like that of a perch. The markings on the body are probably scales. Trout were formerly common in the Mimbres River, but none of the pictures on pottery from ruins in that valley have the adipose dorsal that distinguishes the trout family. There is a considerable variety in the pictures of fishes and probably more than one genus is represented. In no other ancient Southwestern pottery do we find as many different kinds of fishes represented as in that from the Mimbres.

Figure 37 represents a fish with pectoral, ventral, anal, and a single dorsal fin. The tail is uncommonly large. In figure 38 we have a fish accompanied by two birds; the body shows portions of the skin and also backbone and spines. The birds have long legs and necks, which are the structural features of aquatic birds.

In figure 39 we have one of the best examples of Mimbres negative pictures or white on a black background. These negatives are without outlines, their form being brought out by a black setting. Various anatomical structures are evident, as paired pectoral and ventral fins which are curved on one edge; pointed anal fin, small dorsal, crescentic gill-slit, small eyes, no mouth.

Figure 40 represents a sunfish, the body in profile being oval with long pointed dorsal fins and cross-hatched body.

The form of figure 41 is serpentine with two pairs of fins on the ventral side and a single fin on the dorsal region. The body of this animal ends in a fish tail; the head, which is black, has no gill openings in the neck. There is a horn on top of the head which bends forward and terminates in a bunch of feathers. The eye is surrounded by a ring of white dots; teeth white; tongue black.

The small fish represented in figure 42 has three fins on the ventral and one on the dorsal side. Through the whole length of this fish extends a white band, possibly the digestive organs. The fins of this particular fish have spines represented, whereas in other pictures these fins are solid black.

Figure 43 shows two fishes which closely resemble each other in structure. One, however, is painted black, while the other is covered with a checkerboard design. Each of these has a single ventral, dorsal, and pectoral fin, in which regard they differ from the specimens of fishes thus far known in Mimbres designs which commonly have paired pectoral and ventral fins.

Birds.—From their mysterious power of flight, and other unusual characteristics, birds have always been considered by the pueblos to be important supernatural beings and are ordinarily associated with the sky. We find them often with star symbols and figures of lightning and rain clouds. There is something mysterious in the life of a bird and consequently there must be some intimate connection between it and those great mysteries of climate upon which so largely depends the production of food by an agricultural people.

In Mimbres ware, as is usually true in conventional or naturalistic figures on prehistoric pueblo ware, birds excel in numbers and variety all other animals, following a law that has been pointed out in the consideration of pottery from Sikyatki, a Hopi ruin excavated by the author in 1895.[1]

There is, however, a great difference between the forms of birds, conventional and realistic, from different areas of the Southwest, and nowhere is the contrast greater than in those on the fine ware from Sikyatki and that of the Mimbres. The conventional bird and sky band, so marked a feature in the Hopi ruin, are absent in both the Little Colorado and Mimbres pottery.

The wild turkey, one of the most common birds, associated by the Hopi with the sun and with the rain, is repeatedly figured on ancient pottery from the Mimbres Valley.

Figure 44 shows three birds of a simple form from dorsal or ventral side, the head being turned so as to be shown laterally; but generic identification of these birds is difficult.

Figure 45 represents the head, neck, and wing of a parrot. It is instructive as showing wing feathers with white tips and black dots on the extremities. The triangular geometrical figure near its head has six feathers with black dots near their extremities.

Figure 46, one of the most realistic pictures in the collection, is evidently intended for a parrot and is one of the few representations of birds on Mimbres pottery in which the tail feathers are indicated by parallel lines. The special avian feature of this figure is the shape of the head and upper beak, which corresponds pretty closely with

[1] Seventeenth Annual Report Bureau of American Ethnology, Washington, 1898.

a geometric pattern called the " club design " used as a separate design in Casas Grandes pottery decorations.

The appendages on the head of figure 47 are feathers recalling those of quails; the tail is destitute of feathers.

The two wingless birds represented in figure 48 have a characteristic topknot on the head and a highly exceptional bodily decoration. Identification is doubtful.

The bird (fig. 49), shown from one side, has a vertical conventional wing, long neck and legs adapted for wading.

Although the tail of a bird shown in figure 50 resembles that of a turkey, the head and beak are similar to the same organs in a humming bird. Its beak is inserted into the petals of a flower, evidently for honey. The birds (fig. 51), among the simplest figures in the collection, have angular wings, the feathers being represented by serrations or dentations. There are figures of two birds drawn in a white dumb-bell-shaped area in figure 52.

The bird (fig. 53) has outstretched wings with hanging feathers of exceptional form. Legs are not shown, which leads to the belief that the back of the animal is represented. The tail was obscurely shown in the photograph, which made it impossible to obtain a good drawing of this organ. This is one of the few dorsal representations of a bird, most of the others being shown from one side. The position of the hanging feathers of the wings is exceptional.[1]

The bodies of the four birds represented in figure 54 are oval, without wings or legs. Two of these bear triangular and cross designs, and two have lenticular markings. Between the beaks of each pair of birds there is a rectangular and three triangular designs, all terraced on one side.

The tips of the tails of the birds represented in figure 55 are like that of a turkey but it is hardly possible to prove that this is a proper identification.

The bird figure shown in figure 56 exhibits no wing or tail feathers, but the body is prolonged into a point. The head bears four upright parallel lines indicating feathers. Legs, short and stumpy. The object suspended like a necklace from the neck is not identified.

There are several examples of wingless or tailless birds and a few are destitute of legs. The signification, if any, of this lack of essen-

---

[1] On the reredos of the Owakulti altar at Sitcomovi on the East Mesa of the Hopi there is a similar figure with drooping wing feathers. Here it probably represents the Sky god, as there are several stars near it.

tial organs does not appear. Some of the birds have egg-shaped bodies; the heads with long beaks.

Figure 57 probably represents a turkey. The feathers of the tail are turned to a vertical position and the elevated wings have characteristic feathers. The legs end in conventionalized turkey tracks. There is a protuberance above the beak—a well known turkey feature. Figure 58 also represents a turkey, or rather three heads of the same animal with a single body. There are also three wings. The tail is turned vertically instead of horizontally and the claws are four in number—three anterior and one posterior. It has a single breast attachment.

Feather designs.—Among the modern pueblos the feather is one of the most prominent ceremonial objects and the specific variety used in their rites is considered important. Every Hopi priest in early times had a feather box, made of the underground branch of the cottonwood, in which he kept his feathers ready for use. The forms and decorations of Mimbres pottery would seem to indicate that feathers played a conspicuous rôle in the symbolic designs on prehistoric pottery.

The importance of the feather as a decorative motive is somewhat less in Mimbres pottery than in Sikyatki, the symbolism of which is elsewhere[1] considered; but the symbols for feathers in the two areas are different and might very readily be used to distinguish these areas.

The types of the wings and tails of birds here considered were taken from the realistic representations on Mimbres pottery. We often find a dot indicated at the tip of a feather, a feature likewise seen in pottery from Casas Grandes in old Mexico and of wide distribution in aboriginal North America.

In order to be able to demonstrate that a geometrical decoration is a feather in Mimbres designs, the author has taken the representations of the wings and tails of many pictures of birds and brought them together for comparison. A few of these different forms of bird feathers from the Mimbres are shown in the figures (59-92) that immediately follow. The different forms of tail feathers thus obtained are considered first and those from the wings follow. It is interesting to point out that the author's identification of certain linear designs on Southwestern pottery as feathers was not obtained from the surviving Indians but by comparative studies. Starting

---

[1] Thirty-third Annual Report Bureau of American Ethnology, Washington, 1919.

with the thought that certain rectangular designs are feathers, we can demonstrate the theory by its application and association with other bird figures.

Several forms of feather designs that appear quite constantly in the decoration of Sikyatki ware are not found on Mimbres ceramics, and *vice versa*. The Mimbres has several geometric feather designs peculiar to that valley. In the Sikyatki ware the relative number of feathers, free from attachment to birds, used in decoration is larger than in the Mimbres ceramics. Tail feathers have as a rule a different form from wing feathers and are more seldom used. Eleven different figures of birds' tails are here given, and there are twenty-two designs that are supposed to represent wings of different birds.

Tail feathers.—One of the simplest forms of birds' tails obtained in the way above mentioned is shown in figure 59, which represents five feathers. This feather type has square ends, each feather differentiated by lines as far as the body attachment. In figure 60 we also have four tail feathers, but the ends are rounded, and in figure 61 there are four feathers having rounded tips; the two outer could better be regarded as incomplete feathers. There are likewise four feathers in figure 62, but, although the tips are rounded, the angles are not filled in with black as in the two preceding specimens. Here the four feathers are united by a broad black band. In figure 63 three whole and two half feathers are represented, united by two broad transverse bands and four narrow parallel lines also transverse; and in figure 64 there are five whole feathers and two half feathers, which are barely indicated, the lines that divide the two members being simply indicated.

It is instructive to note how often this connecting black band appears on bird tails. Figure 65 is a case in point. Thus far also the feathers of birds' tails considered are about equal in length. Here (fig. 65), however, the middle feathers are longer than the outer; the line connecting the tips would be a curved one.

An innovation is introduced in the tail feathers shown in figure 66. Their tips are rounded and there is a slight difference in general form between the three middle and the two outer members. The novel feature is the appearance of semicircular, or triangular black dots at their tips. Whether the existence of these differences means that another kind of feather is depicted or not the author is unable to say.

In figure 67 the four feathers are characterized by black markings throughout almost their whole length. This variation may indicate a special kind of feather or a feather from a different bird.

Wing feathers.—The simplest forms of wing feathers are marginal
dentations, serrations, or even parallel lines without broken borders.
One of these last mentioned is figured in figure 68, where the wing
is sickle-shaped and the feathers short, curved lines. In figure 69
these lines are replaced by dentations, and in figure 70 we have three
wings, each with dentations on one edge.

The form of the wing has been somewhat changed in figure 71,
but the feathers appear as dentations, while in figure 72 the feathers
have become semicircular, each with a black dot. Wing feathers in
figure 73 are simple triangles without designs, and in figure 74 they
are semicircular figures, black at the base.

Typical forms of wing feathers appear in figures 75-79, which differ
somewhat in form but are evidently the same. One of the essential
features of these wings, as shown in the four figures mentioned, is
their division into two regions distinguished by the forms of feathers
in each case. This is not as well marked in figure 75 as in figure 76,
where the four primary and three secondary feathers on the same
wing are distinctly indicated. The markings on these are similar,
but the primary feathers are long and their extremities more pointed.
In figure 77 we can readily distinguish primary and secondary feathers
in the same wing by the absence of a black marking evident on all
the others, and in figure 78 the three secondary feathers are distinguished by dots near their tips; the primary wing feathers are
here narrower and longer, the longest terminating in curved lines.
Figure 79 represents a wing with seven feathers, of which the four
secondary are distinguished by the existence of terminal dots.

Neither figure 80 nor 81 shows distinction of primary and secondary
feathers but both have blackened tips. A like marking appears in
figures 82 and 83, where it extends along the midrib of four feathers.

Figure 84 represents a right wing of a bird with eight feathers.
A similar representation is found on the left side and for comparative
purposes a cluster of these designs from a bowl decorated with
geometric designs is also introduced (fig. 85).

Three feathers which have markings probably symbolic but different
from any previously described are shown in figure 86. These were
attached to a staff. Their identification is doubtful, which may likewise be said of figures 87 and 88, the two latter being a very simple
form of the feather symbol. The four designs that appear in
figures 89-92 are supposed to represent either tails or wings of birds
in which individual feathers are not differentiated.

It is sometimes difficult to recognize the feather element in some of these and in others it is very well marked. These designs have been identified as feathers mainly on account of their connection with wings or tails of birds.

Insects.—The people of the ancient Mimbres probably did not recognize a sharp line of demarcation between birds and insects. Both were flying animals and can be distinguished in several figures. Figures 93-95 were evidently intended to represent insects, probably grasshoppers. The animal represented in figure 96 is enigmatical. It apparently represents an insect but has strange anatomical features for a member of this group. The head and antennae resemble those of other insects, but the two sets of leg-like appendages, three in each set, hanging from the ventral region distinctly resemble fins of fishes. We cannot identify this as a naturalistic representation of any known water insect. It is probably some conventionalized mythic animal.

It is impossible to identify with any certainty several pictures that occur in the collection further than to recognize that they represent insects. There are several pictures of the grasshopper or locust, and the bee, dragon-fly, and butterfly can be recognized. The object shown in figure 97 looks like an insect but its structure is not sufficiently marked to definitely determine the family.

The insect shown in figure 98 has the wings and extremity of the abdomen similarly marked and recalls the dragon-fly. The head and legs differ considerably from those in figure 97.

Figure 99 appears to represent a moth or butterfly. No identifications were made of figures 100 and 101. Figure 102 is a representation of an animal with four pairs of legs, possibly the insect known as the "skater." It has a head, thorax, and abdomen like an insect, legs like a grasshopper, and a tail like a bird.

The animals, and more especially the geometric patterns represented on both Mimbres and Casas Grandes pottery, are often similar; but this similarity in the beautiful pottery of the northern and southern regions of the Mimbres-Casas Grandes plateau is even stronger than the resemblances here pointed out would seem to indicate. The pottery of both regions, for comparative purposes,[1] may be regarded as belonging to the same area.

---

[1] The northern extension of typical Mimbres pottery is doubtful, but certain food bowls from Sapello Creek, a Gila tributary, bear figures that distinctly resemble those found near Deming. Vide: Hulbert and Watson Collections.

COMPOSITE ANIMALS

One unusual feature of life figures on Mimbres pottery is the union of two genera of animals in composition in one picture, probably representing a legendary or mythological animal. The signification of such a union is not known, as the folk tales of the ancient inhabitants of the Mimbres are unrecorded; but it is instructive to note that similar composite animals are not commonly represented on pueblo pottery, ancient or modern, although we have pictures of reptiles and the like with feathers on different parts of their bodies.

It is also instructive to note how many synchronous differences there are between prehistoric pottery and architecture. While there are evidences of interchange of material objects in two areas, we cannot say that the culture of the inhabitants of any two regions was identical until both have been studied. The occurrence of Casas Grandes pottery fragments in the Mimbres ruins or *vice versa* would indicate that the two cultures were synchronous.

GEOMETRIC FIGURES

The geometric designs on Mimbres pottery are as varied and striking as the life figures, and while they show several forms found on the pottery from Casas Grandes, a large majority are different and characteristic. The geometric decorations are confined for the most part to the interior surface of food bowls, but exist also on the outside of effigy jars and other pottery forms. The geometric designs on Mimbres pottery are not ordinarily complex but are made so by a repetition of several unit designs.

The arrangement of geometric figures in unit designs is in twos, threes, and fours. When there are two different units they are found duplicated. There is seldom more than one unit in the arrangement by threes and very seldom an arrangement of units in fives, sixes, or higher numbers. It is instructive to notice *en passant* that while there are several designs on Mimbres food bowls representing stars, these stars generally have four points, but sometimes five.

Great ingenuity was exercised in filling any empty spaces with some intricate geometric decoration. No two bowls out of over a hundred specimens examined bear identically the same pattern painted on their interiors.

One small but important feature in encircling lines should not be passed in silence. There is no break in decorative lines surrounding the bowl. This is characteristic of the northern pueblo or cliff-house area known as the San Juan drainage, but not of pottery from the Gila basin and the Little Colorado area as far north as old Hopi (Sikyatki). Much of the ancient decorated ware in the area between the Mimbres Valley and the Upper San Juan has surrounding lines broken. The broken line does not occur on the black and white type of ware, of which the Mimbres is a highly modified subtype. From the above facts regarding its distribution it appears that the "line of life"[1] on Southwestern pottery can be traced to southern Arizona, and as black and white ware does not have this feature and is ranked as very old, the decorated pottery of Arizona and central New Mexico where it occurs should probably be ascribed to comparatively recent times. The Mimbres ware has no life line decoration and as this valley is only a short distance from the Gila settlements that show the line of life on their pottery the logical conclusion would be that the Mimbres pottery is archaic or probably older than that which has a life line.

There is at least one ruin in the Mimbres in which pottery with the life line occurs. This pottery is so close in other respects to that of the Gila and so different from that of the majority of neighboring ruins in the Mimbres that we may suppose those who settled there came from the Gila valley.

Underlying the pure pueblo or kiva culture of the San Juan and its tributaries is a prepueblo culture which differs in terms of architecture[2] as well as in various types of artifacts.

The unpolished pottery of the prepueblo culture in the Mesa Verde is distinguished by the varieties of corrugated, coiled and rough unpolished ware. One type has the neck and mouth of the jars formed of coiling while the body of the jar is rough without. Unlike food bowls from the Mesa Verde cliff dwellings, the Mimbres pottery is destitute of painted dots continuous or in clusters that are almost constantly found in this more northern area. The great difference, however, between the ancient pottery of these two regions is of course the absence of realistic figures in the northern and their great abundance in the southern prehistoric ruins.

There are many bowls in the Mimbres ware that introduce areas, triangles, rectangles, and other geometrical figures across which

---

[1] It does not seem probable that this line break originated independently in different ceramic areas of the Southwest. The pottery on which it occurs is supposed to be later than the Mesa Verde.

[2] As elsewhere pointed out, the character of ancient dwellings in the Mimbres belongs to a more ancient epoch than the pueblos; it looks as if the absence of the life line on pottery supported the same theory, but the other features in decoration appear more highly differentiated and therefore more recent.

extend parallel lines or hachures. When triangles, these figures interlock with the same of solid black, leaving zigzag white designs. This is apparently a rare method of decoration of Mesa Verde pottery by indentations, and occurs at intervals down the San Juan to the great ruins of northern Arizona no less than in ruins at Aztec and in the Chaco.

It seems to indicate an older state of culture as it universally underlies the true black and white or prepueblo culture which is missing in the Mimbres, Gila and Little Colorado regions.

While a knowledge of the distribution of the broken encircling line in pottery from Southwestern ruins is not very extensive, those in which it has survived lie in contiguous areas. This feature is absent in the oldest ruins. In the area where pottery thus decorated occurs there survive few inhabited pueblos. Another point: the decorated pottery of the San Juan drainage, where corrugated ware is most abundant, has no life line; this is true likewise with the Mimbres Valley, where the most realistic decorated figures occur, corrugated ware being comparatively rare. The line of life does not ordinarily occur in black and white ware. Archaic ware, generally speaking, has no line of life, which leads me to suppose that the Mimbres ware is older than the Gila pottery. One of the peculiarities of Mimbres pottery is the use of geometric figures on the bodies of animals. These are practically the same as those used free from zoic forms. Their meaning in this connection is not known but several explanations, none of which are satisfactory, have been suggested to account for their existence on animal bodies. This is not common in the pueblo area but occurs in the region or regions that are peripheral in situation, two of which are the San Juan cliff houses and related ruins and the Mimbres; one north, the other south of the central or northern pueblo zone. The author is led to regard this feature as later in development or more modern. If earlier it would probably have been distributed over the whole area. From a study of houses the author was led to believe that the Mimbres settlements were older than the great highly differentiated cliff dwellings and pueblos.

The geographical distribution of the " life line " is suggestive of its comparatively modern origin. It is found in ruins along the Gila and its great tributary, the Salt, in the ruins along the Little Colorado and its tributaries, at Sikyatki, Zuñi and some of the Rio Grande ruins.

The geometrical decorations on Mimbreños pottery can generally be resolved into certain units repeated two or more times, forming a complex figure. We have, for instance, a single type repeated four times, each unit occupying a quadrant. We have also another unit type repeated three times. In a fourth form we have two unit types, each repeated in opposite hemispheres, all together filling four quadrants. In a fifth method we have three different unit types, each duplicated.

In the design represented in figure 103 we have what appears to be a sun symbol or a circle with checkerboard covering and four projecting appendages that resemble bird-tails arranged in pairs, the markings of the opposite members of each pair being practically identical. The geometrical designs on the periphery of the bowl consist of six units, in each of which pure black and hachure are combined. In figure 104 the design appears as a central circle with four radiating arms of a cross, each with checkerboard decoration. Oval white figures alternate with these arms and in each of these ovals is depicted a compound figure of six triangles. A similar design appears on ancient pottery from the Hopi ruin, Sikyatki, where it has been identified as a complex butterfly symbol, and on that from the cliff dwellings of the Mesa Verde. In Mimbres pottery it sometimes occurs on the body of animal pictures, as the author has shown elsewhere.[1]

In the design (fig. 105) a central circle is absent but it has four arms like a cross with zigzag lines. The design (fig. 106) is made up of four S-shaped figures painted white on a black zone. From the inner ring there arise eight radiating lines which extend toward the center. Each of these radial lines has three parallel extensions at right angles.

Figure 107 is a broad Maltese cross painted white on a black background, one edge of each arm being dentated. This figure may be classed among the negative figures so successfully used by the ancient Mimbreños.

A swastica design represented in figure 108 is so intricate that it is not readily described. In the middle there is a square on the angles of which are extensions that have a dentate margin. The designs placed opposite each other are more elaborate than the other four and are triangular with solid colors and hachures.

Four triangular designs radiate from a common center on a white field in figure 109. Serrate marginal edges are used with good effect in this picture.

---

[1] See plates 3, 4, Archeology of the Lower Mimbres Valley, New Mexico. Smithsonian Misc. Coll., Vol. 63, No. 10, pp. 1-53, 1914.

There are two pairs of rectangular designs in figure 110 arranged about a central circle with peripheral serration recalling a buzz saw. The combination of designs surrounding it is unique but the elements resolve themselves mostly into zigzag and checkerboard decorative elements.

The extremities of the cross (fig. 111) are rounded; its arms arise from a central inner circle with figures in white on a black background. Two of the arms are ornamented with terraced rims and two have diamond figures separated by parallel zigzag lines forming bands in white on a black background.

Three pairs of designs can be recognized in figure 112, one pair resembling flowers on stalks; the others, also paired, are octagonal in form, recalling flowers seen from above. An eight-pointed rosette forms the center of one, and a cross, white on black, the other. Six triangular designs in which hachures predominate decorate the periphery.

Two pairs of geometric figures cover the interior of the bowl shown in figure 113. One pair is mainly a checkerboard design, the other chevrons on parallel lines. The central figure is surrounded by nine crosses on a white zone. Figure 114 has likewise two pairs of geometric units arranged about a central circular area which is white.

Figure 115 also has two pairs of radically different units, one with two rectangular designs, the other with wavy lines having dentate borders.

There is a trifid arrangement in the decoration of figure 116, consisting of three lozenge-shaped figures with dentate borders and parallel lines set in as many oval white areas. The central figure is a white circle with black border.

Figure 117 is also made up of three unit figures, each of triangular shape with an elaborate border of solid triangles and hachure surrounding figures.

Figure 118 is a very exceptional decoration and may be divided into six units arranged in pairs. There are four triangles, two pairs of which have a decorated border and two have not, but all alternating with a pair of five needle-like solid black pointed extensions reaching from the margin of the bowl inward. The most conspicuous figure is a unit design consisting of bands with two opposite figures united with the margin by a black line, each decorated with four frets.

Figure 119 is an unique decoration made up of a central circle with five claws like birds' beaks, each with an eye. The interior of each is a five-pointed star.

Figure 120 is a central four-terraced symbol from which extend many radiating feather-like designs. A central rosette in figure 121 has eight petaloid divisions; it is white at the extremities, black at the center.

The decoration of figure 122 consists of an intricate meander filling the peripheral space outside a circular central black area.

In figure 123 the more striking parts are the five white circles, one centrally situated, and four equidistantly placed near the periphery. The main portion of the bowl is covered with figures consisting of rectilinear lines and spirals.

The prominent design in figure 124 is a star with eight slender arms and exceptional peripheral decorations.

The centrally placed design depicted in figure 125 is a quadruped with tail curved upward, recalling a conventional mountain lion. The peripheral figures are of two shapes, lozenge or angular, and semicircular with zigzag extensions.

Two birds stand on an unknown object in figure 126, while in figure 127 we have a quadruple arrangement of parts, the same unit being repeated four times. The most striking designs are bundles of conventional feathers, four in each, arranged at intervals. These have been identified as feathers by a comparison of them with the wing feathers of an undoubted bird elsewhere considered.

The designs shown in figures 128 and 129 are four-armed crosses. Between the arms of the last mentioned figure there are white designs on a black ground.

Now and then we find in ancient Mimbres pottery the universal symbol called the swastica. Figures 130 and 131 are geometrical, the latter having three instead of four arms. Figure 132 represents a four-armed swastica in which the extremities of the arms are quite complicated.

One of the most beautiful geometric designs from Mimbres pottery is shown in figure 133, where a combination of curved and linear figures, black, white, and hachure work, all combine to produce the artistic effect. Elsewhere [1] the author has figured a similar design with four S-figures around the periphery of a bowl.

The design on the food bowl shown in figure 134 is very ornate and in a way characteristic of Mimbres ware. We have in its composition solid black, hachure, and white rectangular lines and scrolls

[1] Archeology of the Lower Mimbres Valley. Smithsonian Misc. Coll., Vol. 63, No. 10, pl. 8.

so combined as to give a striking effect and attractive harmony. Of all geometric figures this appears to the author to be one of the most artistic.

In figure 135 is an artistic combination of a double ring of terraced triangular figures surrounding a central zone in white, and in figure 136 there is a composite decoration composed of a complex of triangular designs. In figure 138 there is a white square in the middle, around which are arranged eight figures of two kinds alternating with each other; four in each type.

The design in figure 137 is simple, consisting of a number of white zigzag figures with intervals filled in with triangles, sometimes black and sometimes crossed by parallel lines.

In figure 138 we have two groups of similar unit designs, four in each group, composed of triangular blocks terraced on one side and crossed by parallel lines. The simple designs on figures 139-140 need no elaborate description.

CONCLUSION

The material here published is extensive enough to permit at least a preliminary estimation of the relation of Mimbres pottery to that of the so-called pueblo area on the north and that of Casas Grandes on the south.

The Mimbres valley is an ideal locality for the development of an autochthonous and characteristic ceramic area. There is not sufficient evidence to prove that decorative elements in any considerable number from the North modified it to any great extent, for we find little likeness to pottery of the Tulerosa and other tributaries of the Gila and Salt. The pottery of the Mimbres had crossed the watershed and reappears in the sources of tributary streams that flow into the Gila. Examples of it have been found on Sapello Creek, which, so far as we know, is the northern extension of the Mimbres culture. The beautiful pottery collected by Mrs. Watson at or near Pinos Altos clearly indicates that Mimbres pottery was not confined to the Mimbres Valley. Limited observations often render it impossible to trace the extreme northern extension of the Mimbres pottery, but it seems to grade into ceramics from the upper Gila and Salt River tributaries. The southern migration of pueblo pottery appears to have been very small, but, elements of foreign character worked their way into the Mimbres from the west, as is clearly indicated by shards from the ruin at the base of Black Mountain.[1] The line of demarcation between the two on the west is clearly indicated by specific characters.

The Mimbres pottery most closely resembles that from the Casas Grandes mounds in Mexico, on the south, but whether we may look to the south for the center of its distribution is not apparent. The mounds near Casas Grandes River are situated in the same inland plateau, and although Casas Grandes pottery excels the Mimbres in form and brilliant color, it is inferior to it in the fidelity to nature of its realistic pictures of animals. In this respect the Mimbres has no superiors and few rivals.

We have found no evidence bearing on the antiquity of Mimbres pottery from stratification. It is not known whether it overlies a substratum composed of corrugated, coiled, or black and white ware as commonly occurs in the pueblo and cliff-house regions. Decorative features characteristic of it have been developed independently in this isolated region. A knowledge of the length of time required for its development as compared with that necessitated for the evolution of the Sikyatki designs must await more observations bearing on this subject.

The animal designs were not identified by Indian descendants of those who made them. A determination of what they represent is based solely on morphological evidence. They are as a rule well enough drawn to enable us to tell what animal they represent. Very often the animal is recognizable by comparisons, for we can reconstruct a series reaching from a symbol made with a few lines to a well drawn picture. There is danger in supposing that a series thus constructed may always lead to accurate identifications as comparisons of symbols with decorative designs are often very deceptive.

The break in decorative lines surrounding pueblo food bowls and other forms of pottery is absent in specimens from the Mimbres Valley. This is also true of the cliff house and other pottery of the San Juan Valley.

Pottery from the Gila basin and the intervening area as far north as old Hopi ruins has this life line. Much of the ancient decorated ware found in the area between the Mimbres valley and the upper San Juan also have surrounding lines broken.

[1] The author has already commented on this infiltration in his Archeology of the Lower Mimbres, *op. cit.* Mimbres and Casas Grandes pottery are readily distinguished.

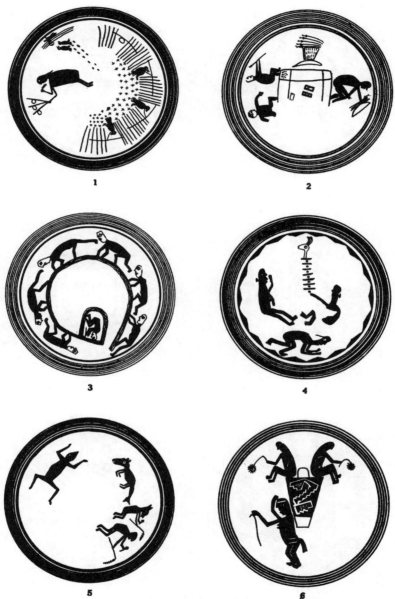

OSBORN COLLECTION.

1. Snaring wild birds.
2. Game of chance.
3. Men emerging from the underworld.

4. Man shooting off the lightning.
5. Two men and two animals.
6. Two men and one woman.

OSBORN COLLECTION.

7. Two men kneeling on quadrupeds.
8. Two men lying on table.
9. Two men with bodies and limbs of animals (Hulbert collection).

10. Man dancing.
11. Two men dancing and two turkeys.
12. Two human figures.

13   14

15   16

17   18

OSBORN COLLECTION.

13. Man representing plumed serpent, cutting off head of a victim sacrificed.
14. Two carnivorous animals.
15. Quadruped (probably wolf).

16. Two men dragging a quadruped.
17. Horned composite quadruped with feather head-dress.
18. Man with rabbit ears and body.

OSBORN COLLECTION.

19. Two animals in white, resembling
    beavers.
20. Unknown quadruped (mountain lion?).
21. Rabbit.

22. Negative pictures of two rabbits.
23. Two rabbits.
24. Rabbit.

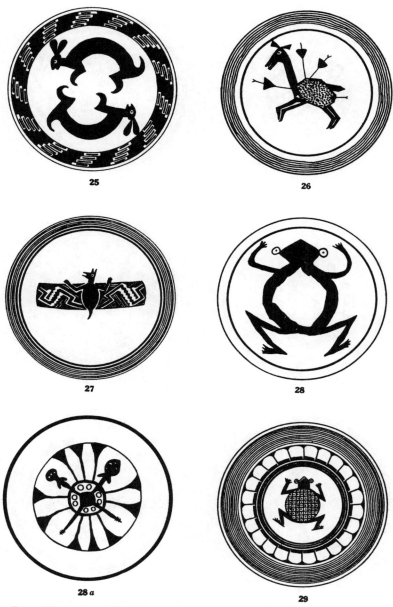

25. Two rabbits surrounded by a zone containing thirteen bundles of feathers (Hulbert collection).
26. Unknown animal (Osborn collection).

27. Bat (Watson collection).
28. Frog (Osborn collection).
28a. Tadpoles (Osborn collection).
29. Turtle (Osborn collection).

30

31

32

33

34

35

30. Turtle (Osborn collection).
31. Turtle (Osborn collection).
32. Snake talking to a mountain sheep (Osborn collection).
33. Two lizards with white outline (Osborn collection).
34. Lizard (Hulbert collection).
35. Two lizards talking to a crane (Osborn collection).

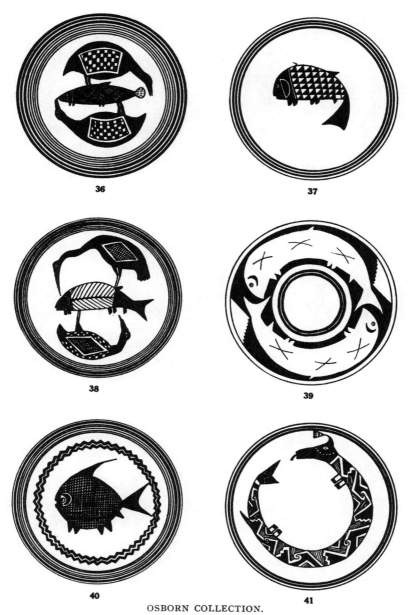

OSBORN COLLECTION.

36. Fish with two birds standing on it.
37. Sun fish.
38. Two birds standing on a fish.

39. Two fishes drawn in white on black ground.
40. Sun fish.
41. Serpent-like monster with horn on head.

OSBORN COLLECTION.

42. Coiled fish (Hulbert collection).
43. Two fishes symmetrically arranged.
44. Three birds.

45. Parrot.
46. Well-drawn parrot.
47. Quail.

OSBORN COLLECTION.

48. Two birds on dumb-bell-shaped field.   51. Three birds.
49. Bird with wings extended.   52. Two birds with triangular tails and wings.
50. Two birds taking honey from flowers.   53. Sun bird.

OSBORN COLLECTION.

54. Four birds with swollen bodies.
55. Two birds with long necks.
56. Unknown bird.
57. Turkey.
58. Turkey with three heads.

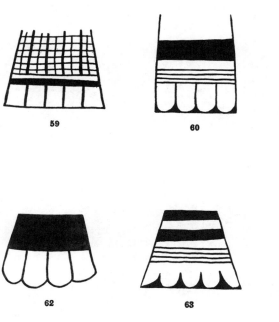

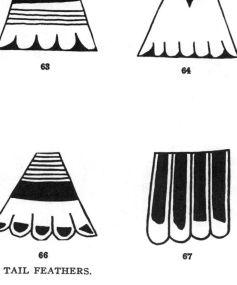

TAIL FEATHERS.

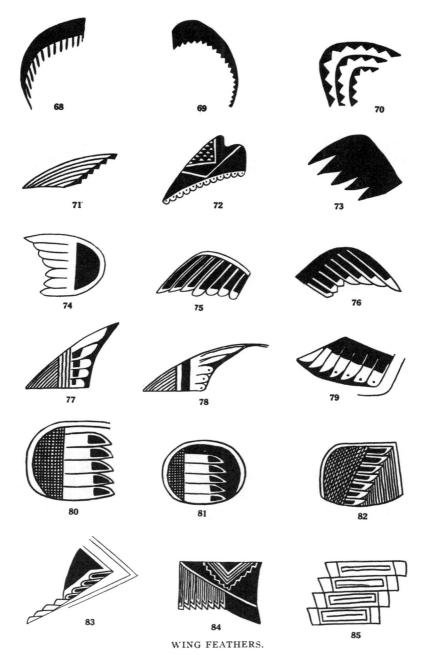

WING FEATHERS.

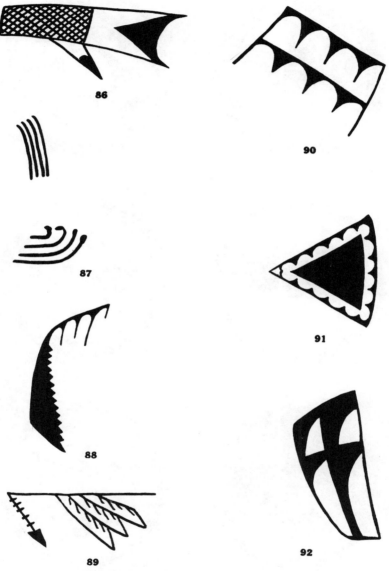

ABERRANT WINGS AND TAILS OF BIRDS.

OSBORN COLLECTION.

93. Grasshopper with extended wings.
94. Four grasshoppers with extended wings.
95. Locust.

96. Unknown animal.
97. Unknown animal.
98. Dragon fly.

99. Butterfly (Hulbert collection).
100. Unknown animal (Osborn collection).
101. Insect with extended wings (Osborn collection).
102. Water bug (Osborn collection).
103. Sun emblem (Osborn collection).
104. Cross with butterfly symbols (Osborn collection).

105   106

107   108

109   110

OSBORN COLLECTION.

105. Cross painted white, alternating with
    four zigzag lines.
106. Geometrical figure with friendship
    signs (Hulbert collection).
107. Maltese cross, modified.
108. Rectangular figure, modified.
109. Cross.
110. Cross with zigzag modifications.

OSBORN COLLECTION.

111. Cross with rounded arms.
112. Six flowers, two in profile, the remainder from beneath.
113. Geometrical figure.
114. Geometrical figure.
115. Two-armed rectangular figure.
116. Center circle with three rectangular figures with serrated edges.

117

118

119

120

121

122

117. Swastica with three points (Osborn collection).
118. Figure of unknown meaning (Watson collection).
119. Five heads of birds around a central circle (Osborn collection).
120. Radiating feathers (Osborn collection).

121. Radiating pear-shaped objects surrounded by elaborate zone of complicated solid black and parallel lines (Osborn collection).
122. Figure of unknown meaning (Osborn collection).

123

124

125

126

127

128

123. Intricate design with five white circles (Hulbert collection).
124. Star with eight rays (Osborn collection).
125. Quadruped surrounded by zigzag lines (E. White collection).
126. Two birds on an unknown weapon (Osborn collection).
127. Cross with four bundles of feathers (*vide* fig. 53) (Osborn collection).
128. Rectangular cross around a circle, with elaborate peripheral design (Osborn collection).

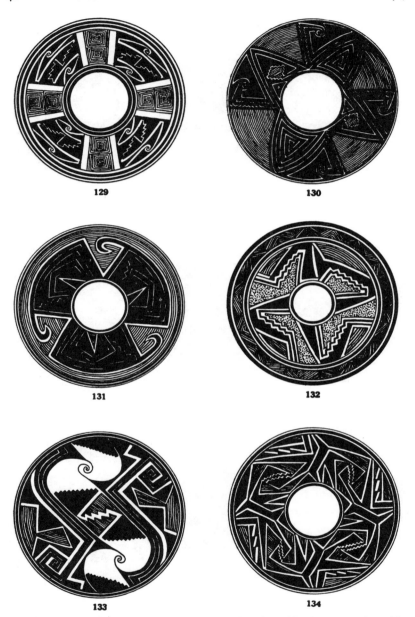

129

130

131

132

133

134

129. Maltese cross (Osborn collection).
130. Cross with arms of two types (Osborn collection).
131. Three-pointed swastica (Osborn collection).
132. Swastica with zigzag extensions (Osborn collection).
133. Combination of rectangular and spiral designs (Osborn collection).
134. Complicated unknown figure (Watson collection).

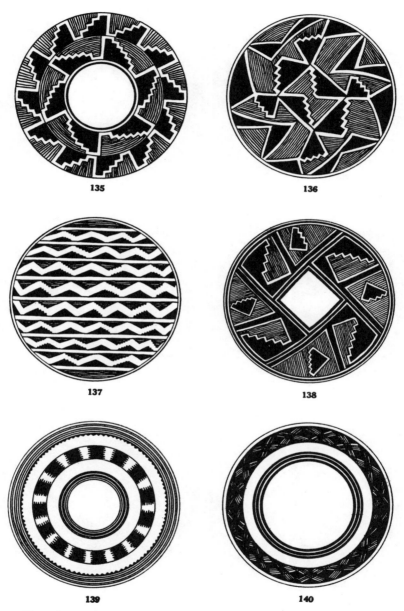

135
136

137
138

139
140

135. Rings of cerrated symbols surrounding a central white area (Watson collection).

136 to 140. Geometrical ornamentations of unknown meaning (136, 138, Watson collection; 137, 139-140, Osborn collection).

ADDITIONAL DESIGNS ON PREHISTORIC
MIMBRES POTTERY

Avanyu Publishing Inc.

SMITHSONIAN MISCELLANEOUS COLLECTIONS
VOLUME 76, NUMBER 8

ADDITIONAL DESIGNS ON PREHISTORIC MIMBRES POTTERY

BY
J. WALTER FEWKES
Chief, Bureau of American Ethnology

(PUBLICATION 2748)

CITY OF WASHINGTON
PUBLISHED BY THE SMITHSONIAN INSTITUTION
JANUARY 22, 1924

ADDITIONAL DESIGNS ON PREHISTORIC MIMBRES POTTERY

By J. WALTER FEWKES

CHIEF, BUREAU OF AMERICAN ETHNOLOGY

INTRODUCTION

In former papers [1] the author has tried to show, from archeological studies, that the prehistoric aborigines of the Mimbres Valley, New Mexico, developed a culture area differing from any other in the Southwest. The characters which more than any other distinguish this culture from others are the adornment of food bowls with realistic, sometimes composite, figures of men and animals, and the artistic character of the designs. Previously to the year 1914, few prehistoric Mimbres picture bowls had been published, but since that date, as shown in part by the literature,[1] many of these have been brought to light, and there are now several collections of size from this valley, which have characteristic realistic figures. Of late years there has been considerable activity in collecting prehistoric pottery in this area, and in May and June, 1923, the author revisited the Mimbres Valley to procure some of this new material for the U. S. National Museum, and the following paper is mainly devoted to descriptions of specimens purchased at that time from Mr. E. D. Osborn, who first called his attention to the pottery of the Mimbres Valley.

There are also considered in this article copies of photographs and drawings of other designs and specimens which could not be purchased for the U. S. National Museum.

The collections of Mimbres pottery that have been examined in the preparation of this article are: about 100 specimens from the Osborn collection, which were purchased; the collection owned by Mr. R. E. Eisele, of Fort Bayard, New Mexico; the collection made by Mrs. Watson, of Pinos Altos; and that of Mrs. Hulbert of the same city. Mr. and Mrs. Cosgrove allowed the author to inspect a fine collection carefully made by them at Treasure Hill (Whisky Creek) near Silver

---

[1] Archaeology of the Lower Mimbres Valley, New Mexico, Smithsonian Misc. Coll., Vol. 63, No. 10, 1914. Designs on Prehistoric Pottery from the Mimbres Valley, New Mexico, *ibid.*, Vol. 74, No. 6, 1923. Vide, *idem.* Vol. 65, No. 6, 1915; also Amer. Anth. (N. S.), Vol. XVIII, pp. 535-545, 1915.

City. This collection is particularly valuable as it was obtained from one ruin. The author also examined a few small collections, as that of Dr. Swope, previously considered, and a few specimens belonging to Mr. Thompson, of Deming.[1]

Although this article is limited to designs on pottery, which are by far the most distinguishing feature, the Mimbres culture may also be characterized by other artifacts which will be considered in a final report on Mimbres prehistory.

Mimbres pictures are painted on the interiors of food bowls and the exteriors of vases. These objects are mortuary and found under the floors of the rooms, the walls of which nowhere rise above the surface of the ground, but are readily observed as small piles of rock called Indian graves. The grave yards are situated along both banks of the Mimbres River and are almost in sight of each other. In its course after it emerges from the hills the Mimbres River sinks underground but flows onward, reappearing at times when the clay bed of the river rises to the surface. The ruins do not always follow the subterranean course but occur scattered over the plain.

Although the geographical extension or horizon of the Mimbres area, as indicated by its peculiar pottery, has not been carefully worked out it is practically limited to the Mimbres Valley, but not necessarily to the terraces along the river. There are sites with picture pottery on the eastern side of Cook's Peak, a prominent mountain belonging to the range that incloses the Mimbres basin on the east. Northward Mimbres pottery has been found over the continental divide in ruins on Sapillo Creek and tributaries of the Upper Gila. The western extension of the Mimbres pottery area is not known, but the ceramics rapidly change in character in this direction, merging into Gila Valley types.

While the designs figured and described in this paper enlarge our knowledge of the ancient Mimbreños they do not materially change conclusions already published. Before we can attempt any very extensive interpretations we sorely need more material; but with the information here published we may venture a few suggestions regarding the culture of the ancient Mimbres people. This knowledge, being wholly derived from archeological data, must from the nature of its source be tentative. We have no other way of revealing the manners and customs of this prehistoric race, as historical accounts are very

---

[1] The author takes this opportunity to thank all those who have aided him on his visits to the Mimbres, especially Mrs. Watson, Mrs. Hulbert, and Mr. Eisele, who have allowed him to photograph and publish specimens in their collections.

meager and no one has identified the survivors of these people. Archeology contributes knowledge of their life by means of objective material and for that material we must search among wrecks of their houses and the mortuary and other objects which are found in them or in their graves and refuse heaps.

No one has yet carefully excavated their buildings sufficiently to determine the form of their rooms, although fragments of walls have been brought to light. There are two types of mounds, differing in size and contents. One of these types, situated at the Gonzales Ranch, is lenticular in form, made up of adobe containing few stones. These mounds appear as low elevations rising but a few feet above the surrounding surface. The other type, which seems to belong to a later settlement, is indicated superficially by piles of stones formerly laid in adobe in walls of rudest masonry. These walls formed rooms united in rows or even inclosing square courts. In some places there appear on the surface circles of stones,[1] generally of small diameter, bearing outward resemblances to the tops of the bounding walls of buried ceremonial rooms or kivas. Circular kivas have not been found, up to the present, as far south as the Mimbres but a knowledge of their existence and structure would be of value in comparative studies. Subterranean walls extending far below the surface have been laid bare, and several of these have a fine plastered surface.[2] Little is known of the structure of the roofs as wooden beams have not yet been found. The floors are composed of hardened adobe, sometimes overlaid with flat stones. The dead were buried in the corners of the rooms below the floors, some with limbs extended, others flexed. The bowls that accompany the dead are variously placed, some being at the side of the dead, but now and then they were placed over the head like a cap. Mortuary bowls were deposited with the dead by the ancient pueblos, whose cemeteries are situated outside the walls of their villages. These clusters of stone houses are locally called Indian grave yards, and are generally situated on natural terraces a few feet above the river bed to avoid inundation, but are not confined to the banks of the river, often appearing miles

---

[1] Possibly ceremonial rooms. "Architecturally the prehistoric habitations of the Mimbres Valley represent an old house form widely distributed in the Pueblo region or that antedating the pueblo or terraced-house type before the kiva had developed."—Arch. Mimbres Valley, p. 52.

[2] Mr. Cosgrove (El Palacio, July 16, 1923) identifies two rectangular rooms excavated by him at "Treasure Hill" as kivas, and refers to ventilation in them. The author is unable to accept this identification without more knowledge than is now available of their structure.

away from springs, suggesting the puzzling question, " Where did they get water? " One of the largest of the ruins, situated on Montezuma Hill, in sight of the highway not far from the village of Pinos Altos, covers a high hill and consists of many clusters of rooms. In no instance is there evidence that the rooms of Mimbres houses were several stores high or terraced as in the pueblo region. Neither has excavation revealed buildings surrounded by a wall resembling compounds like Casa Grande in the Gila. The mounds of ruins are low, seldom if ever having walls projecting above ground.

The most instructive of the large Mimbres ruins, and one that has yielded many specimens, is called Old Town. This site gives every evidence that it was once a populous settlement. It is situated at the point where the Mimbres river leaves the mountains and enters Antelope Valley. Old Town is a typical Mimbres ruin but has been pretty well ransacked by pot-hunters, yielding some of the most interesting specimens from this valley.

REALISTIC DESIGNS ON POTTERY

The designs on Mimbres pottery are mainly painted on the inside of food bowls and naturally fall into three groups: (1) Realistic; (2) conventional; (3) geometric. The large majority are realistic figures of animals. There are several realistic birds' figures where wings or tail have become more or less conventionalized. The geometric figures either form a marginal decoration or cover the whole interior of the bowl. They often adorn the bodies of animals.

There is one interesting group of realistic designs that is unique in pueblo decoration, viz., parts of two animals united, forming a composite representation of some mythological personage.[1] In one or two instances human bodies have animal heads supposed to be masks.

The different designs collected in 1923 are considered in the following pages. The most exceptional figures are those of composite animals, one of which is shown in figure 1, drawn from a photograph. This bowl, owned by Mr. Eisele, was found by him on the Gonzales ranch. The main figure was evidently intended to represent a human being crouched in a sitting posture, annexed to which is apparently the body of a bird, as shown by tail feathers. The face of the human being is well made and the body wears a kilt of checkerboard design. There are two curved pointed horns on its head. The face is crossed

---

[1] In this connection see Tello, Las representaciones de los dioses en el arte antiguo peruano. Inca, Vol. 1, No. 1, January-March, 1923.

by a white band; body and limbs are black. The author believes
that here we have a composition of human figure and the tail of a
bird, quite different from any figure on any other piece of pottery
known to him.

One of the most instructive pictures in the Eisele collection is the
bowl shown in figure 2, upon which are represented three butterflies
with outspread wings, two with extended and one with retracted
probosces. Each butterfly has two wings around the edge of which
are the customary dots which are almost universally found on butterfly
figures from the Hopi to the Gila Valley. In the middle of this group
stands a man who carries on his head a small vase which he holds in
position. One of the butterflies, clinging to the elbow of the man
by its feet, extends its proboscis as if to take the contents of the
vase. The color of this vase is light cream and the figures are painted
in brown merging into black. The ordinary symbol of the butterfly
is, of course, triangular; but in this case we have this insect shown
from one side, which is a very rare position in pueblo pictography.

The design on figure 3[1] is very intricate, consisting of two units,
each twice represented at opposite ends of diameter of the bowl.
These units may be called central and peripheral. The former represent two human beings facing in opposite directions and separated by
geometrical figures. The arms in each case are raised above the head
as if holding a burden. The face of one is white; the color of the
body is black. The appendages are slim. The other or peripheral unit
is thought to represent a bird. Each of the two representations of
this unit has extended tail. The last joint of the legs and the attachment of the legs to the back suggests a grasshopper. This is one
of the most complex of all the Mimbres figures, and probably illustrates some ancient myth of which there is no survival, as the aboriginal
inhabitants of the Mimbres have either completely disappeared or,
what is more likely, have been absorbed into other stocks.

Figure 4 represents a native drawing of a naked[2] human figure
with a feather tied in his hair. He holds at arm's length, in both hands,
an animal which resembles a snake. On first sight the impression
would naturally be that this figure indicates that the prehistoric
Mimbreños had some form of a snake dance, like that of the Hopi,
or that this figure represents a shaman or snake charmer conjuring
with a reptile. It calls to mind a figure holding a curved object which

---

[1] When not otherwise stated specimens here described are now in the collection of the U. S. National Museum, and were purchased from Mr. Osborn
in 1923.

[2] Naked men's bodies and limbs are painted black.

might be either a rabbit stick or snake, shown in figure 5; but until we have more detailed material we cannot regard this as more than a suggestion. It does not, of course, follow, even if this man is carrying a snake, that there was an elaborate snake dance among the Mimbreños.

Figures of snakes are rare, but Mrs. Watson, of Pinos Altos, has a bowl with two coiled designs resembling snakes but without an accompanying human figure; the author has elsewhere[1] figured a horned snake from this region.

The posture of the well-drawn figure of a man in figure 6 (Eisele Collection) is peculiar. Arms and legs are extended and the upper part of the head and nose is black; cheeks white.

The two human beings shown in figure 7 are remarkable. They suggest a child riding on the back of his parent, holding on literally by the hair of his head. This interpretation does not explain the fish attached to the nose of the smaller figure, leading to the belief that there must be some unknown legend back of this figure. The fish has the two ventral fins and the two pectorals. There is also an anal fin but no dorsal. The fins that are represented are longer and more pointed than is usually the case; and the crescent that ordinarily represents the gill opening and operculum is missing, its place being occupied by an unusual black object depicted on a white ground.

The small figure is apparently clothed in one of those jacket-like garments worn by figures of hunters shown in a former article.[2] This garment is held in place by a woven belt whose ends appear in the figure, tied around the body. There is no indication of clothing on the larger figure, whose head, body, arms and legs are black, the customary color in representing nude figures. The attitude of the arms suggests an ancient Egyptian at prayer. The profiles of the faces in both figures have a certain likeness.

Whether figure 8 represents fishermen who have captured a large fish, some fish legend or a ceremony connected with fishing, is unknown, but each of the four participants has a line connected with the fish's mouth and above the group is an upright pole with feathers attached at intervals. Every man has a different attitude and the faces of all are painted white with black crowns. The cheeks are crossed with parallel lines which also extend lengthwise on the fish. The operculum

---

[1] Archaeology of the Lower Mimbres Valley, Smithsonian Misc. Coll., Vol. 63, No. 10, fig. 28, 1914.

[2] Archaeology of the Lower Mimbres Valley, Smithsonian Misc. Coll., Vol. 63, No. 10, fig. 13, 1914.

is not crescentic as in most fishes but is indicated by a white line. The head, fins, and tail are black; ankles of all men are white in color.

In figure 9 a man holding a bow and arrow is shown; head and limbs are evident, but the bowl is so broken that other details do not appear.

The head of the animal represented in figure 10 resembles that of a carnivorous animal, as a mountain lion. The remarkable feature in this figure is the tail, which is very much thickened and elongated, bearing a terraced design on the surface and ending in a triangular tip. A chevron figure on the head of this animal has some resemblance to one on a serpent figured elsewhere.[1]

The design figured on the inside of the food bowl (fig. 11) represents a quadruped with a very long tail, curving over the back and ending in a white tip. Attention should be called to the fact that in this figure the anterior legs bend forward, and not backward, which is the general case in most quadrupeds. This animal is apparently walking on his tail and perhaps visualizes some ancient myth similar to one to which my attention has been called as existing among the Plains Indians.

The quadruped depicted in figure 12 evidently represents some carnivorous animal of the cat group, resembling somewhat a wolverine. The interior of the bowl was so much broken that only one figure remained, the duplication being restored.

Figure 13 is a figure of a mountain sheep or goat not unlike some other representations of the same animal elsewhere figured.

We have in figure 14 a representation of a mountain goat, the form and attitude of which is highly characteristic. In figure 15, which represents a mountain sheep, the differences are brought out.

Figure 16 represents a mountain lion but differs from any yet figured in the white line that extends from the ears to the throat. The tail in this figure is turned over the back—an almost universal position in pueblo pictures of the mountain lion.

Figure 17 is a negative picture, or one in white on a black background, representing a rabbit. The ears bear the customary black spots, and the eye is circular in form.

Figures 18, 19, each represent two rabbits painted black on a white ground. The body of one is marked with a longitudinal curved white band with black dots, the other with a checkerboard pattern. But few instances of rabbit pictures are known to me in which the side of the body is decorated with any figure.

---

[1] This figure has, however, a cephalic horn which is absent in the design considered, which also has two ears.

In figure 20 we have representations of two animals, possibly mother and offspring, one large, one small, both of which have similar projecting jaws. The posterior end of the body of the smaller merges into a fish; the body and hind legs of a quadruped are replaced by the body and fins of a fish, two on the back (where there is never in other fishes more than one dorsal), and one anal fin.[1]

Figure 21 shows two hornless quadrupeds standing feet to feet on an ornamented base decorated with checkerboard design. The body of each bears an intricate cross design with stepped edges. The neck has white lines on three sides of a rectangle. Body black; eyes lozenge shaped; ears prominent; tail short, stumpy, marked with white lines.

Figure 22 represents some mythic animal with four legs, and a raised wing. The body is continued in a very unusual posterior appendage recalling a human leg. This specimen belongs to the Hulbert collection. The body is surrounded by a belt with two series of squares, alternating black and white. The mythologic conception in the mind of the painter of this design is a strange one, unlike any yet described in pueblo folk tales.

Figure 23 represents two figures with round heads, large white eyes and prominent lips. The figures of hands apparently are shown on the corners of the bodies. Legs well drawn and toes human in character. No suggestion is made regarding the identification of these figures.

Figure 24 is a negative picture of a flying creature like a bat[2] with large outspread wings, round head like that last mentioned, and prominent ears. This animal has a tail like that of a mouse outlined in white on a black ground.

Figure 25 shows two quadrupeds with short, stumpy legs, relatively large heads and small necks, with white bodies. No identification of these animals has been made and the details of the small drawings are very incomplete.

The peripheral parallel lines surrounding these figures are crossed by a zigzag line which follows the course of the inner cluster of encircling parallel lines making a singularly ornate and exceptional decoration.

---

[1] The frequent occurrence of fish designs on Mimbres picture pottery has led to a suggestion that we have evidence of a former life near more water than now flows in the Mimbres. But facts do not warrant the conclusion. The author has previously described a figure of a combined antelope and fish.

[2] The belief that this figure represents a flying mammal or bat, is based on the shape of the head and the absence of feathers.

Figure 26 belongs to the Eisele collection and was found in the same ruin as figure 1. It represents a wading bird (ibis ?) with correspondingly long legs and neck, along which are four small fishes. A short distance from its beak is another fish, apparently about to be devoured by the bird.

One of the instructive forms of composite animals is a figure resembling a bat seen laterally. It shows tail, fore and hind legs of a quadruped, and an appendage attached to the back as seen in figure 27. This appendage represents a wing or row of feathers, seven of which are rounded at the tips and 24 marked with dots at the distal end, and three have their extremities cut off straight, angular or more pointed than the other feathers. The snout of this animal closely resembles that of a bat and has teeth. Three arrows are shown as converging at the mouth as if talking to this animal. Altogether, this is one of the most exceptional forms of flying animals in the Eisele collection, and represents some ancient myth.[1]

As in collections previously described, avian figures predominate, but the few specimens here considered introduce one or two novel variations. The simplest form of bird figure in the collection made in 1923 is shown dorsally in figure 28. Here we have a form where wings, body, tail, and head are outlined with straight lines. The head is triangular, black in color, with two dotted eyes. The wings are also triangular and are crossed by parallel lines. The body is rectangular and the tail ends in two triangular black points. The peripheral zone of decoration of this vessel is peculiar and artistic, consisting of alternating zigzag and triangular lines, the character and shape of which are shown in the figure.

Figure 29 (Eisele collection) represents a quail with tufted head turned to one side, and peculiar wing feathers. The aborigines rarely represent a bird laterally with its head twisted back as gracefully as in this picture. The curved appendage to the eye recalls the club-shaped bodies so constantly occurring in Casas Grandes pottery. The wing feathers are of two varieties: one with rounded tips and dots; the other pointed, without dots. The wing is made conspicuous by being white in color while the body is black. The necklace is white.

---

[1] It suggests a quadruped with an extended wing of a bird. The situation of the arrows is suggestive. In several Hopi legends there are accounts of how a supernatural being shot arrows into the sky, which talked with a mythological personage and then voluntarily flew back to the sender. One of these talking arrows was noted in the legend of the Snake people. Snake Ceremonials at Walpi, Journ. Amer. Arch. and Eth., Vol. IV, 1894.

The bird in figure 30 has widely extended wings of triangular shape. the feathers being represented by dentations on the lower side; the tail feathers have characteristic white tips. The body is globular, without legs. There are parallel lines on the head resembling a tuft of feathers. The body decoration is a square enclosing three parallel concentric lines and a white interior. The head is turned to one side, but the tail is shown from above.

Figures 31 (Eisele collection), and 32 are representations of a similar bird. The extended wings of figure 31 are crescentic and bear midway three parallel white lines. Along the lower edge of each wing are clubshaped feathers. The head and tail are seen dorsally. The legs are abnormally extended, one on each side. The irregular design just below the neck is a perforation made when the bowl was " killed."

In figure 33 we see a well drawn representation of a turkey cock, showing the tail feathers twisted vertically out of perspective. The figure below on which it stands is a turkey hen. We have here both sexes of the turkey. It will be noted that the body of the cock is not perfectly square but the surrounding lines are slightly bent or curved, imparting some grace to an otherwise stiff figure.

As has been stated elsewhere negative pictures of animals or geometric designs occur on both Mimbres and Casas Grandes pottery. In these figures the animal is not drawn but a background is painted in such a way that a white figure is represented. In certain Mimbres designs within the profile of the white or rectangular field is a picture in black. A figure of a human being or animal drawn inside the negative of the same is exceptional in pueblo ceramic decoration. An example of this form of design is shown in figure 34.

The bird represented in figure 34 is double headed and is one of those very exceptional figures in which we have a negative picture overlaid with a positive so that the latter seems to be rimmed with a white border. The body is rectangular, covered by a checkerboard design of small black and white lozenge-shaped figures. The two wings are dentated along their borders; legs short, without claws. The two round heads with short beaks face in opposite directions, and curved appendages recall feathers.

Remove the picture in black from its setting or background and the negative picture of a bird still remains, or a white figure with black background. There are one or two other examples of similar overlaid pictures in Mimbres picture bowls.[1]

---

[1] Designs on Prehistoric Pottery from the Mimbres Valley, Smithsonian Misc. Coll., Vol. 74, No. 6, fig. 10, 1923.

A well drawn bird figure shown in figure 35 is represented on the right side. Unlike most of the Mimbres birds its beak is short and the legs are small, placed far back on the body. Almost all the body is covered by a checkerboard design composed of alternate squares, white and black in color. The extended primary and secondary feathers of the wing are clearly seen. The tail is quite unlike that of other birds, more like that of some quadruped. The geometrical marking on the body under the extended wing is exceptional.

The design on the bowl shown in figure 36 is an unknown bird whose neck is ornamented with a number of dotted squares arranged in a zigzag figure recalling the design on the head of a Horned Serpent shown elsewhere. The association of the checkerboard figure on the sun and serpent symbol is highly suggestive. The puncture in the middle of this bowl hides the figure on the body which is indicated by ends of white lines. This bird stands above an implement of unknown use.

Figures 36a to 36f represent the different forms of this implement which is several times figured with the realistic designs from the Mimbres. The exact use of these objects is not known but it has been conjectured that they were knives, batons, or other stone objects, with handles. The simplest form is shown in figure 36a and consists of an elongated blade attached to a handle. This blade has zigzag markings which Mr. De Lancey Gill has suggested represent chipping of a stone implement (" sword ").

Figures 36b and 36c are aberrant forms of an implement that may have been used for defense, the same shown under a bird in figure 36. Figure 36f resembles in some respects a stone spear point.

Figure 36a introduces a figure of a circular body between the handle and the shaft, and two crescentic extensions between the handle and the blade.

Figure 36e would seem to be analogous to the group of implements above although it wants the handle so conspicuous in the three preceding figures. It has a circular extremity around which are a number of small semicircles. This object was held in the hand of a quadruped, whereas, the other objects were associated with birds.

In figure 36f, where two of these objects are represented on the same bowl, we have, in addition to the handle, radiating lines at the point of attachment of the shaft and handle.

The middle of this bowl has been punctured in " killing," thus rendering it impossible to discover whether an arm and leg is drawn on each side.

As the use of the objects which these figures represent is purely conjectural it is much to be hoped that other bowls on which they may be figured will later be brought to light for examination.

The present figure (fig. 37) is from the original now in the U. S. National Museum, and differs from the former illustration[1] in the tail feathers which are unique. Each of the six tail feathers bifurcates into two parallel lines as here shown (fig. 37). The wing is highly symbolic; its central part in the original has a brown color which is here incorrectly indicated by parallel lines resembling hachures elsewhere shown. We have only one-half of this bowl, but there were undoubtedly two parrots on it when complete. The triangular object in front of the parrot is connected in some way with the " sword " elsewhere considered.

Portions of a head and tail of an animal are shown in figure 38. Enough is preserved to indicate that they are parts of a bird figure carrying a twig of leaves or feathers in the mouth. The middle of the bowl is too much broken to enable one to determine the shape of the body, wings, and the remainder of the design.

The mouth of figure 39 has teeth unlike any genus of living bird and the tail resembles that of a fish more than any other animal. The specimen is owned by Mr. Eisele, of Fort Bayard. The head bears two horns that remind one of some species of Cervidae, but the body and wings are strictly avian. The correlation of a long neck and legs exists in this picture.

Figure 40 shows two negative designs, that above representing a rabbit and the one below a highly conventionalized bird. These two figures are separated by a band consisting of several parallel lines black and white alternating. The original is in the Hulbert collection at Pinos Altos.

Figure 41 is a well drawn bird from the Eisele collection as seen from the side. This bird shows a tail prolonged at the two corners into pointed feathers and is the only bird design that has this characteristic.

Figure 42 represents a man herding a turkey whose globular body is different from that of any turkey yet described. The original specimen is in the Watson collection at Pinos Altos.

Two designs of figure 43 in Mrs. Watson's collection are supposed to represent serpents, but their identification is doubtful. They are comparable with the so-called serpents held by the priests shown in figures 4 and 5.

---

[1] Designs on Prehistoric Pottery from the Mimbres Valley, fig. 46. Fig. 6 in this article is a female figure with a basket on her back in which are twins, each with a sun symbol.

Figure 44 is the dorsal view of a lizard. The design on the margin of this bowl appears never to have been completed but consists of triangles, five of which are simply outlines; the remainder filled in with solid black.

The surface of the food bowl shown in figure 45 is decorated with a picture of a turtle crowded into the whole interior surface of the bowl. The body of this turtle is crossed by a number of parallel longitudinal lines and on each side of it are two curved bands with dentations on one side. The hind legs have no indications of feet. On each side of a pointed tail and in a corresponding position to the head there are depicted angular extensions of the rim, black in color, the shapes of which can be seen in the figure (45).

The head of figure 46 also resembles that of a turtle but the fragments of the bowl on which the body was drawn are missing. The fore and hind legs and tail are represented by triangles painted solid black.

Figure 47 represents a turtle with outstretched legs, triangular head and a single eye. It is surrounded by four white scrolls.

Figure 48 has fragmentary parts of two lizards arranged side by side.

Figure 49 represents a turtle with four claws; the tail and head shown on the periphery of the carapace. The back is covered with a rectangular figure with concentric quadrangles.

It is interesting to notice how often [1] the fish was used by the prehistoric aborigines of the Mimbres Valley in decorating the inside surface of their food bowls. The main differences in the different fishes are specific or indicated by the geometric figures on their bodies or in the shape and number of their fins. The body of the fish shown in figure 50 is decorated with a plaid, rarely used but not unknown as a geometric ornament.

Animals with their mouths approximated are sometimes found on Mimbres ware and it is suggested that the intention was to represent these two animals as talking to each other. In figure 51 we have a common example of this usage in Mimbres pictography, namely, a bird and fish with mouths approximated.

Figure 52 represents a fish, the body of which is covered by a checkerboard design of alternating black and white squares. In other respects this figure is not exceptional, similar fishes having been often

---

[1] Very few fishes are depicted on prehistoric pueblo pottery of other areas so far as is known to the author.

figured, but the arrangement of the gill opening is unusual and the anterior end of the body is differently marked from others that the author has seen.

The bowl, the design on which is shown in figure 53, was broken when found, rendering the relationship of the two animals and the accompanying object painted on it more or less doubtful, but parts of a fish figure and of an antelope are recognizable. The highly instructive original of this picture is owned by Mrs. Watson. Apparently this is not a composite of an antelope and fish but the former stands in front of the latter. The author has no theory to suggest regarding an identification of the object on which the hind legs of the antelope rests.

The animal pictured in figure 54 is called the " vinagaroon " and belongs to the Arachnida, or spider group, differing from Insects in having four pairs of legs instead of three. Two representations of this animal are known to the author but the greater part of one figure is illegible.

Figure 55 represents some insect, as a grasshopper, the surface of the body of which is covered with a checkerboard pattern.

The animal shown in figure 56 has three legs on one side of the body, recalling an insect. It has antennæ and head like those of the same group of animals; but the body is far from realistic, recalling a turtle. This may be one of the composite animals of which the author has already spoken, as its identification as one animal is difficult.

The design on figure 57 represents the same animal as figure 56, but with minor differences. Legs are absent in this figure and its body instead of being decorated with a checkerboard pattern has wineglass and other figures in white outlines on a black ground. In figure 57 the semicircular design corresponding to the curvature of the body is black; its middle is occupied by a semicircle with hachures and saw-toothed straight edge.

The author is unable to identify the insect pictured in figure 58. It has certain anatomical likenesses to the ant lion but the head is somewhat exceptional. The original figure shows a possible composite animal, but the relationship of it is unknown. The original is owned by Mrs. Hulbert, of Pinos Altos.

Figure 59 is probably a mythological conception, the identification of which is at the present time conjectural. In form the main design is a prominent circle with triangular extensions suggesting a sun symbol and two eyes like those of a mask. This disk is supported on two appendages resembling legs. An elbow-shaped organ hangs between these legs, and the region of the face below the eyes is covered by a chevron-shaped zone of alternate black and white squares forming a checkerboard decoration reminding one of the figure of the sun elsewhere shown. It is possible that this is a representation of some mythological being, or symbol associated with sun worship; but too little is known of the Mimbreño mythology to properly identify it.

GEOMETRICAL DESIGNS

The Mimbres geometrical designs are quite unlike those described from pueblo areas. Several geometric designs are negative figures or white designs brought out by black backgrounds. The most abundant geometric figures are the interlocking slanting terraces, one covered with hachure, the other plain black. In all the figures rectilinear lines predominate and zigzags are the most pronounced. It is wonderful how many different designs can be produced by a modification of the two interlocking terraces, parallel lines and cruciform figures. All geometric designs are limited to the inside surface of mortuary bowls, the exterior being destitute of decoration. There are no broken encircling lines.

The characteristic geometrical patterns of the Mimbres ware, on account of their strictly American character no less than their great artistic beauty, are particularly good as patterns for decoration of fabrics and specialists have already begun working on them with this thought in mind. They are as unlike those of prehistoric pottery from other pueblo areas as are the various realistic designs already considered. Their significance cannot be determined—a condition true of most pueblo geometric figures—but irrespective of that they are of the utmost importance in determining by comparative methods of the relations of the pottery and hence the relation of subcultures of our Southwest which is the home of the pueblos. The general characters of the geometrical patterns may be seen in figures 60 *et seq.,* no two of which are identical. It will be seen on examination of these figures that the majority are linear designs with now and then curved lines. Among other figures may be identified the cross, stars, broad arrow, squares, triangles, checkerboard and other figures.

The designs are simple, either covering the whole interior surface of the food bowl or confined to the periphery leaving a central circular, rectangular or other formed area without decoration.

The design on figure 61 represents a four-pointed star outlined in pure black and filled with a hachure. Its center is occupied by a geometric figure with a number of concentric smaller rectangles

A five-pointed star has not yet been found in Mimbres designs and the star made up of four blocks of solid black with a white center so common on Sikyatki[1] (a Hopi ruin) and other Hopi pottery is likewise absent in Mimbres ware.

In figure 62 we also have a representation of a star verging into a cross in which the arms are not pointed but cut off at right angles. The design in figure 63 is cruciform with suggestions of a swastica. The arms are prolonged into needle-like points; on one side of each arm there are three serrations with notched edges. This unique form of cross the author does not find duplicated in prehistoric pueblo pottery and is peculiar to the Mimbres.

The cross-shaped figure forming the design (fig. 64) has three arms and a central circular area; the intervals between the arms being filled in with parallel lines or hachures and dots. This figure, like the preceding, is peculiar to the Mimbres ceramic area.

There is very little duplication of geometric designs in the collection. The design of figure 65 is painted red and consists of three arms, each formed of three parallel lines extending from a circular center to the periphery. The three areas between these groups of lines are filled in with zigzag white figures ending in interlocked spirals, a unique form of decoration.

In figure 66 we have the negative picture of a three-lobed design bordered with dentations, the triangular intervals being filled in with solid black.

The beautiful design shown in figure 67 can best be appreciated by an examination of the illustration. Cross hatching introduced in the two opposite units is a new feature in Mimbres geometrical designs and is exceptionally striking.

There are six white bordered arrows in figure 68 alternating with three rectangles with hachures and three in white forming an attractive design exceptional among pueblo decorations.

Figure 69 is an artistic design with four rectangular figures on a black ground alternating with which are eight small white circles each with a cross in black at its center.

Figure 70 is largely made up of negative designs artistically arranged with hachures, dual terraced figures forming a combination of a unique character in pueblo designs.

Figures 71 and 72, hitherto undescribed geometrical decorations on pueblo pottery, are artistic and so far as known characteristic of the Mimbres. Although the various geometrical designs on Mimbres pottery differ greatly they have a general similarity.

[1] Vide 17th Ann. Rep. Bureau of American Ethnology.

Figures 73 and 74 are characteristic designs not found among pueblos.

The design on figure 75 is an intricate serrate figure surrounding a central circle that is devoid of decoration. The two regions of the zone about the central figure are different; on one side we have three points of a star; on the other bars and hachures.

The design shown in figure 76 is a central white circular zone with projecting points of an irregular star around which is a meander of white lines with black background, in four zones, each zone remotely like the others.

Figure 77 has zigzag lines surrounding a central circle without decoration. There are rain-cloud designs which can best be seen by examining the figure.

In figures 78 the design is composed of zigzag and other figures surrounding a central undecorated circle.

Figure 79 shows a design on a black background made up of zigzags, rectangles, and hachured triangles surrounding a central undecorated zone.

Figure 80 recalls pueblo designs but is strictly characteristic of the Mimbres.

Figure 81 is an unusual geometric pattern in which hachures and white zigzag lines predominate.

In figure 82, representing a design from the Black Mountain ruin, we notice the main differences between Gila and Mimbres designs. This bowl is made of red ware and has a yellow interior on which are painted a solid black circular rim and white squares with black dots.

In order to show how much the designs on Gila Valley pottery differ from those of the Mimbres Valley the author has introduced figure 82 from the Black Mountain ruin not far from Deming. This ruin was settled by colonists from the Gila Valley and in its mounds are also found other specimens of Gila Valley pottery as well as that characteristic of Casas Grandes, specimens of which are also shown in subsequent figures.

The design (fig. 83) consists of a number of zigzag bands radiating from the center.

Each of the designs (fig. 84) can be reduced to a quadrangular body the margins of which have rows of triangles.

The design on figure 85 is stellate, in which the white is brought out into a negative picture by a decorative black base. The design is not symmetrical and is characteristic.

In figure 86 we have represented a design made of white areas as in figure 85 forming a cross with four arms. Few specimens of this design have been found in the Mimbres Valley.

The design (fig. 87) has elements of figure 86 and that shown in figure 88 has an hourglass center. The last designs are unique, never found in pueblo decorations.

Figure 90 shows a unique design from a Mimbres bowl composed of two units: one, white bars interlocking with parallel black lines; the other, white zigzags on a black base.

The design on the food bowl shown in figure 91 is a cross formed of white bands, and parallel lines surrounded by encircling lines and hachures arranged in groups.

The design on figure 92 may be reduced to two rings surrounding a black central circular region. These two rings are made up of alternating white triangles on a black ground; but these triangles do not correspond, to form rectangles, as one would expect; the triangles in the interior zone are more pointed than those of the exterior zone. There seems to be no indication, however, that in making these double designs a pattern was used, and the whole design affords evidences of having been drawn free-hand.

In figure 93 we have a design depicted on a flat circular clay disk, in Mrs. Watson's collection, slightly curved on one face and flat on the other. The design is restricted to the curved surface; the flat side being undecorated. The use of this object is unknown, but it has a likeness to one shown in profile in a previously published figure where three men engaged in a game of chance are represented and the stake is a bunch of arrows in a basket.

Figure 94 shows a design of intricate character in which are introduced a central undecorated area surrounded by a rectangular figure with radiating extensions recalling figure 63. The peripheral portion of this design is quite different from those previously described in the so-called friendship curve, a pueblo feature repeatedly found on pictographs and pottery designs. It also occurs in various modifications of Mimbres pottery.

Figures 95 and 96 are simple designs that need no description and can be readily understood by examination of the illustrations. The element of artistic beauty in figure 95 that separates it from the majority of other designs of the same general nature is a series of dotted lines forming a tracery passing over the zone of parallel lines surrounding the central figure.

Figure 97 shows two effigy jars from the Mimbres Valley which are instructive as indicating the geographical distribution of this form. In the Casas Grandes pottery, where these effigy jars are much more numerous and complicated, we have a very large relative number of similar forms, some of which have been modified into human figures. In the Mimbres, on the contrary, objects of this kind are quite rare. The designs on the two here figured strictly belong to the Mimbres group.

In figure 98 we have still another of these effigy jars, which, however, differs from those spoken of above in that a handle is absent. The form of these jars suggests a conventionalized bird, the conventionalized designs on the body representing wings; the eyes and mouth are rudely indicated by circles. The remaining designs on figure 99 are representations of a mountain sheep, and on figure 100, what appears to be a composite animal having a tail of a bird and the limbs, thorax, body, and head of an insect.

The last figure (fig. 101) represents four rude undecorated vases belonging to the coiled variety of pottery, evidently cooking vessels, one of which has a handle. This type of pottery, found throughout the Mimbres Valley, recalls the archaic types recorded from the pueblo region but is crude in comparison with them. It resembles somewhat prepuebloan types from northern New Mexico and Colorado, but the fine corrugated and coiled ware of the North is thinner and shows greater technique and variety than that either of the Mimbres or Casas Grandes in Chihuahua.

Geometric decorations are generally arranged on bowls either in two or four; sometimes in three, but very rarely five and higher numbers. When the unit design is doubled the two units are placed diametrically opposite on the bowl. Decoration is always absent on the exteriors of the food bowls. It will be noticed in a consideration of dual designs in the series that the repetition of the same unit is painted freehand; no pattern or stamp was used and the unit pattern when repeated varies somewhat in execution. Evidently the potter held the object in her hand and painted by the eye, arranging the figures in such a way that the spaces might be filled by the pictures. A modification of the shape of the figure to conform with the area to be covered was not uncommon. The lines are sometimes so fine that we can hardly suppose the chewed end of a yucca stick was used as a brush as is generally the case among the Hopi.

COMPOSITE DESIGNS

The composite pictures are representations of two animals combined. The custom of uniting different animals as a unit is sometimes found among the more advanced tribes of Mexico and Central America, but is rare or unknown among the North American Indians. As examples of these composite pictures may be mentioned quadrupeds represented with a human head and nondescript animals with the body of an antelope and tail of a fish, or tails of twin fishes added to a turtle body. These composite pictures illustrate to the Indian mind their folk-lore or mythology and may represent mythological beings or legends now forgotten which were current at the time they were made. It may be possible by renewed research to find survivals of these stories in the folk-tales of kindred peoples and thus determine what personages these composites were intended to represent; but at present we can do no more than recognize that the Mimbres Valley pottery bears evidences of a rich mythology or folk-lore that has disappeared. Fishes and quadrupeds are the most common of the composite forms.

Two of the best examples of a composite animal in the collection now being described are shown in figures 1 and 14; in figure 37 the wing and its feathers, also the tail feathers, are conventionalized, while the head and body of the bird are wonderfully realistic.

Attention may be called to the tendency to conventionalize certain organs, as wings and feathers of birds, even when the figure of the bird is realistic. This may be an index of the change from realism to symbolism which in Sikyatki pottery has gone so far as to reduce the whole figure to a symbol.

COMPARATIVE STUDY OF MIMBRES DESIGNS

Geographically the valley of the Mimbres lies between high lands on the east and north and the Casas Grandes Valley on the south. As the physiography of these neighboring areas is different and pottery designs unlike each other, it may be well to devote a few lines to comparative studies. The northern and western neighbors of the aborigines of the Mimbres were those of the Gila Valley and its tributaries; on the south the Mimbres Valley merges into that of northern Chihuahua. It is natural that the distribution of ancient pueblo and other pottery in our Southwest should follow rivers or streams of water whose banks are natural trails. The presence of water, also a desideratum for an agricultural population, may be considered in a general treatment of migration of people.

The geographical location of tributaries of four streams of constant water, the Gila, the Rio Grande, the Little Colorado and the San Juan, played an important part in migration. The Mimbres not being connected with these rivers or their drainage areas, being in a way isolated, we may expect, *a priori,* that its pottery was little modified by that of these other drainage areas. The Rio Grande river in the latitude of Deming to the Gulf of Mexico is singularly free from tributaries, especially on the right bank, and there are no river routes for interchange of prehistoric people. Higher up we find pueblos on this river still inhabited. The Gila river also has few tributaries in its lower course and few ruins away from the river itself. It runs east and west; its sources and those of the Salt divided into numerous tributaries. In this country of the Upper Gila and Salt we find many ruins of several varieties. There are several northern tributaries where ruins are abundant and in the Upper Gila there are many tributaries and many ruins among the canyons of the sources of this river. Throughout its whole course from source to the Gila Bend there are many ruins. The northern tributaries overflowed their population beyond the Mogollon into the Valley of the Little Colorado as far north as the Hopi, Zuñi, *et alii.* This wide north-south distribution of Gila Valley pottery is due to the direction of the flow of the many tributaries of these rivers.

The main tributaries of the San Juan on the left or south bank were also significant in the direction of human migrations. The general trend of migration is south from this river and the ruins are more abundant near the sources and along tributaries. The isolated Mimbres Valley migrations had very little effect on the pottery designs of the aborigines of the San Juan.

There seems to be a consensus of opinion of the few ethnologists who have considered the Casas Grandes ceramic culture area that it is true puebloan, or that pottery likenesses are sufficient to place both in the same group. If we limit the term " true pueblo " to a type of sedentary culture [1] that developed in the northern part of New Mexico and Arizona and the southern part of Utah and Colorado, the differences are striking. The author believes there are so many features in the culture of the Gila that are different from the pueblo that in strict scientific usage it is better not to classify them in the same type. .

It is believed that the Gila culture spread north over the Mogollon mountains into the Little Colorado valley and even north of that into

---

[1] Practically the so-called " Kiva culture " of the San Juan Valley, whose structural characteristics have been elsewhere pointed out.

the Hopi region where it mingled with the true pueblo, migrating southward, thus forming a mixed culture. In New Mexico the same thing happened; the pueblo element, originating in the north, extended as far south as Zuñi, in which are evidences of a mixture with the Gila culture. The ancient potters of the Upper Gila and Salt rivers left abundant pottery and there is enough material from which we can by comparison determine their relation to the people of the Lower Gila. They show the union of the true pueblo culture and that of the aborigines south of them, which did not greatly differ from the pueblos.

The pottery of the adjacent Gila-Salt area differs from that of the Mimbres in several characters. The designs on the interior are broad black rectangular lines on a gray surface, the outside of the bowl being red in color, whereas Mimbres ware is white with narrow black or red figures [1] on the inside of the bowls.

It is also pertinent to point out the differences between the pottery of the Mimbres Valley and that of northern Chihuahua (Casas Grandes region), which are significant. The available collections thus far made in these two regions afford differences in data; an examination of these collections shows that the specimens from the Mimbres are food bowls, while those from northern Chihuahua are vases. As a rule food bowls found in the latter region are small and deep, although sometimes large. They are decorated on the exterior, which is not the case in similar vessels from the Mimbres. About ten per cent of the Cases Grandes vases are effigies, while only a very small portion of the Mimbres vases can be so designated. In the Casas Grandes area are many polished black bowls like the so-called Santa Clara ware, but little black ware has thus far been found in the Mimbres. The same is true of undecorated red ware, which occurs in Chihuahua but is rare or absent in the Mimbres.

It is mainly in the decoration of pottery of the two areas that we find the greatest differences in the pottery. That from the Chihuahua mounds is more brilliant in color than any other in the Southwest; it is very smooth without superficial slip, in which it recalls old Hopi ware from the ruins of Sikyatki where the beautiful figures are also painted directly on the surface, not on a slip. Casas Grandes ware is a polychrome, or red and yellow on a gray-white ground. The ware

---

[1] Incidentally attention should be called to the uniform width of the encircling parallel lines and the boldness with which they are drawn in Mimbres ware. In the accompanying figures Mrs. Mullet has preserved that uniformity in breadth of line and distance apart. This fact is mentioned lest some critic may find too much regularity in the drawings.

from the Mimbres may be called the black and white, although many
of the bowls are gray rather than white, and even pass into a red.
The decorations of both Casas Grandes and Mimbres [1] food bowls are
drawn in black and brown ranging into tan color, but it would appear
at times as if this difference in coloration was due to unequal firing of
the paint which is apparently some iron oxide. There are one or two
polychrome bowls and one in which the figures are decidedly red.
The change in color by exposure to the air in some specimens which
were collected in 1914 is perceptible. But while the Mimbres pottery
may be classified as black and white ware it differs from that found
in cliff dwellings and other archaic ruins. The main differences are
not so much in colors as in designs, which afford a clear idea of
cultural differences. In other words, it is, of course, in the decorations that the main difference between the pottery from the two
regions lies.

The animals represented on the Chihuahua (Casas Grandes) pottery are very few compared with those on Mimbres ware. Birds,
snakes, a quadruped or two, the frog, and one or two others, embrace
the main animal designs on the southern pottery, while in the Mimbres
the number of animals depicted in very much larger. A complete list
of these would make a catalogue of some size, but a few of those
animals not found on Casas Grandes ware might be mentioned.
Among quadrupeds are the lion, deer, antelope, mountain sheep; several species of fishes; a large number of birds; many insects, as
butterflies, dragon flies; scorpions, turtles, lizards, and various other
animals. None of these are represented in relief, however, as is the
case with animal forms on pottery from Casas Grandes, but are
painted on a flat surface mainly on the inside of bowls. There is no
area in the Southwest where the animals represented on pottery out-
number those of the Mimbres, nor any area where the aboriginal
potters have left us such truthful realistic pictures of animals by
which they were surrounded.

The representations of human beings in the Chihuahua ware are
painted effigies; there are few representations, so far as known, of
an effigy human being or one in relief on the pottery of the Mimbres. The author has seen no picture on Casas Grandes pottery in
which men are represented as hunting, gaming, or engaged in any
occupation.

---

[1] The character of the design rather than the technique of the pottery distinguishes the two regions.

The geometrical designs as well as naturalistic representations of men or animals from Casas Grandes and the Mimbres have much in common but several differences. One of the most common of the geometrical decorations is the step figure divided into two halves separated by a zigzag band. This is almost universal throughout the pueblo area.[1] In the Casas Grandes ware one of these oppositely placed series of step figures is generally (not always) black and the other tan colored or red. The same design on the Mimbres ware has one series painted a solid black color and the other has hachure lines, a design which occurs all over the Southwest and which the Mimbres area shares with the Pueblo and the ruins in the valley of the Gila. This likeness suggests that the Mimbres ware is allied both to the puebloan and to that from Casas Grandes.

One important geometrical decoration of the Mimbres pottery consists of parallel lines. In their desire to decorate all portions of the object they have almost invariably filled in different geometrical outlines with hachure or cross hatching, checkerboard or other rectangular figures as suited the wish of the designer. Another favorite geometrical design is the cross of various kinds, among which the elaborate swastika may be mentioned. A rectangular design of frequent use throughout the Southwest is the compound triangle made up of two or more united triangles. This is a favorite decoration on the bodies of animals and has been variously interpreted. The triangle is the symbol of life, and the arrangement of several triangles may have some similar meaning. Similar triangles, double or single, appear on the walls of kivas or sacred rooms of cliff dwellings, in the houses and on the wedding blankets of the Hopi girls. Among the living Hopi a triangle is commonly said to represent the butterfly, a symbol of life or fertility.

Another favorite rectangular ornament is the checkerboard pattern, alternate clusters of black and white triangles or squares forming a very effective rectangular pattern. The checkerboard is very commonly associated with the sun but is also frequently found in the paintings of animal bodies.

The majority of geometrical figures are rectangular or triangular: Spirals, circles, and curved lines are very rare.

There is one geometric design which occurs almost universally in the pueblo area and while it suffers several modifications is essentially identical in widely separated geographical localities. This dec-

---

[1] One of the strongest reasons advocated to include these areas among the pueblos.

oration may be called the " dual reversed stepped design." It is composed of two terraced figures so placed that their terraces interlock, leaving a zigzag line between them. This is particularly characteristic of black on white or gray ware which is most abundant on the oldest decorated pottery of the Southwest, but it also survived into modern times. In the Mimbres pottery as in other types it forms the most abundant form of geometric decoration. The two series of reversed terraces are different either in color or design. This is indicated in the Mimbres by solid black on one side and hachure or parallel lines on the opposite, while in the Casas Grandes pottery one series is solid black, the other red, hachure being exceptional; the terraces here, acute angled among the pueblos, become right angles as in Mesa Verde pueblos situated in both caves and open situations.

The presence of this " dual reversed stepped design " on the ancient decorated pottery of our Southwest in the judgment of some authors relegates both Mimbres and Casas Grandes pottery to the pueblo type. It suggests that the Mimbres pottery is old,[1] and the fact that it is so abundant on black and white ware, which is considered old, supports the same conclusion. There are several other characteristic pueblo designs on Mimbres pottery, as the interlocked spiral. They point to pueblo affinities.

The rectangle is found constantly on pueblo pottery; it is sometimes simply an outline but may be solid black or crossed by parallel lines which may be cross hatched and form a checkerboard pattern with or without dots. The edges of these rectangles may be dentated, serrated, or without ornament, simply plain. The rectangular figure, generally single but rarely double, is very common on animal designs.

The realistic figures on Mimbres and the symbolic figures on Sikyatki[2] ware have little in common; there are comparatively few realistic animal designs depicted on bowls from the latter ruin. It was the habit of the Sikyatki potters to decorate the outside of their food bowls as well as the interior with geometric figures, a habit rarely if ever practiced by the Mimbres potters. The highly conventionalized designs on the inside of Sikyatki food bowls were seldom

---

[1] The black and white ware found elsewhere in the Southwest shows very few realistic figures except in the Mimbres, but many simple geometric designs.

[2] 17th Annual Report, Bureau of American Ethnology, Pl. CXXI. While comparative studies bearing on the relation of Sikyatki pottery are not wholly satisfactory it has seemed to the author that the affiliations of Awatobi designs with those of Sikyatki are not as close as he thought a quarter of a century ago. Awatobi pottery is nearer to that of the Little Colorado than is Sikyatki, and this is also the teaching of tradition.

accompanied with geometrical figures. Negative pictures, so common on the Mimbres ware, are not found on ancient Hopi (Sikyatki) ceramics. The great difference between ancient Mimbres and Hopi designs is that the former are realistic [1]; the latter conventional and limited to a few forms; no fishes, turtles, or deer appear on Sikyatki ware because aquatic animals were absent from their water course. Among the cliff houses we find mountain sheep represented realistically as pictographs. The ceramic art of Sikyatki reflects a waterless desert, but the Mimbreños lived in a valley where water, although small in quantity, was perennial.

The " killing " of mortuary bowls before they were buried is almost universal in Mimbres ware. The bowls were almost without exception perforated artificially. Sometimes several perforations were made and in one instance three of these holes were arranged in such a way as to suggest a mask with the mouth and eyes of a human face. Sikyatki pottery was never perforated and " killing " mortuary objects was almost wholly unknown. There are no reliable evidences that the San Juan cliff dwellers killed their mortuary pottery. The potters of the Gila killed their mortuary vessels as did also certain of their descendants.

The Mimbres pottery is distinguished from that of Casas Grandes by significant conventionalized designs. The " club-like " ornament, so conspicuous a negative design on Casas Grandes decoration, is practically absent in the Mimbres area. This ornament can generally be reduced to bird heads, feathers, or even bird bodies, and is generally introduced to fill in triangles where the background is solid black. Whereas bird figures on Casas Grandes ceramics like the " club-like " figures are almost invariably negative or white on black background, only a few negative pictures of birds are found on Mimbres ware, but instead birds are black or red painted on a white ground; we have no human beings, fishes, rabbits and other animals in white on black in Mimbres ware. This is one of the several differences between the pictured pottery of the two culture areas. Although bird figures differ there is a similarity in the form of feathers when used as an individual decorative element in the two regions.

We can say that the remarkable development of realistic designs in the Mimbres area is local, but that the designs are related to the pueblo and have affinities on one side to the Gila and on the other to the Casas Grandes, but on the whole the culture was self centered

---

[1] At Sikyatki we find few realistic and many symbolic and geometric designs; in the Mimbres many realistic, few symbolic and many geometric.

and unique. The interlocked terraced figures and spirals it shares with the pueblo may be a survival of a pueblo relationship and may be an evidence of a remote kinship, but in the Mimbres environment the designs have become wholly unlike the northern relatives.

RELATIVE AGE OF MIMBRES POTTERY

The age of the Mimbres Pottery is unknown save that it antedates the historical epoch. The method of determining its age by the stratification of shards in refuse heaps has not been found feasible in this region, mainly because deep refuse heaps have not yet been discovered. The small size of those that are known indicates a rather short occupation and although a few different kinds of pottery occur they have not yet been arranged in an evolutionary series. It is doubtful whether or not all types were synchronous with the picture bowls. Probably when the valley was first peopled the colonists came from areas beyond the mountains and the production of realistic figures developed after they had inhabited the Mimbres Valley for some time.[1]

The fact that these designs are highly realistic or specialized does not, in the author's judgment, mean that the culture which they express was necessarily late in development. What few facts we have point to limited residence in an isolated valley.

The potters who painted the designs on Mimbres ware were contemporary with those who decorated the beautiful pottery of northern Chihuahua and that of the Gila compounds as indicated by the presence of shards or even complete specimens from these regions. The transfer was either by traders or possibly by clans or colonists seeking new homes, which appears to account for the alien ware at Black Mountain ruin.

While the penetration of the Casas Grandes type of pottery into the Mimbres Valley, either through trade or otherwise, is indicated by this ceramic distribution, we have no evidence of a counter migration or that Mimbres types or styles of design migrated south across the Mexican border. We have large collections of Casas Grandes ware but in none of them are true Mimbres picture bowls.

The great abundance of designs and the absence of conventionalism is interpreted to mean that pottery making in the Mimbres was not

---

[1] Unfortunately the individual ruins from which most of the specimens here considered have been taken are not definitely known. There is, however, no evidence that there is any great difference in age between the various ruins along the Mimbres.

limited to a few individuals as among the Hopi. Many Mimbres women were potters and there was more individuality in the designs they used. Among the ancient Hopi (Sikyatki) pottery designs show a more crystallized conventional art.

It is not possible in the present state of our knowledge to determine the date when the prehistoric Mimbreños disappeared or possibly were merged into the Apache of the same time, but it appears that they were contemporaneous with the prehistoric population of the Gila and the Casas Grandes.

MIMBRES FOOD BOWLS.

1. Human being with horns.
2. Man and three butterflies.
3. Two human beings and two animals.

4. Man with serpent.
5. Man with snake.
6. Seated man.

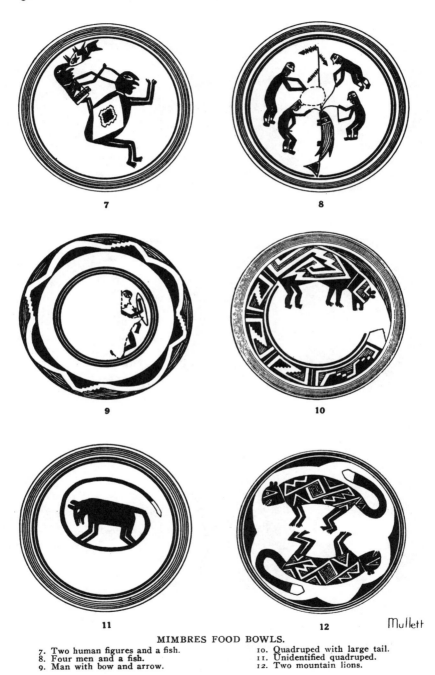

7

8

9

10

11

12   Mullett

MIMBRES FOOD BOWLS.

7. Two human figures and a fish.
8. Four men and a fish.
9. Man with bow and arrow.

10. Quadruped with large tail.
11. Unidentified quadruped.
12. Two mountain lions.

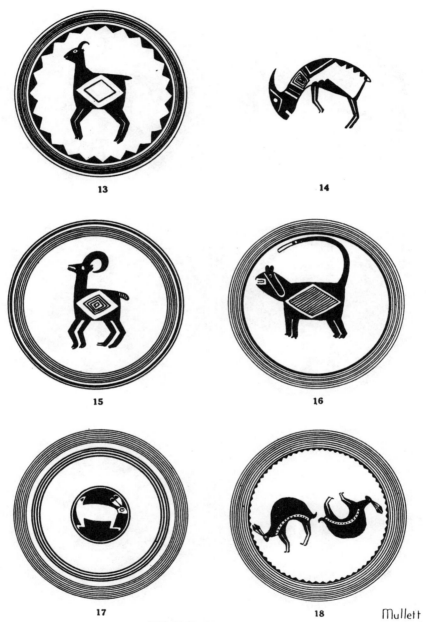

MIMBRES FOOD BOWLS.

13. Mountain sheep. 16. Mountain lion.
14. Mountain goat. 17. Negative picture of rabbit.
15. Mountain sheep. 18. Two rabbits.

3

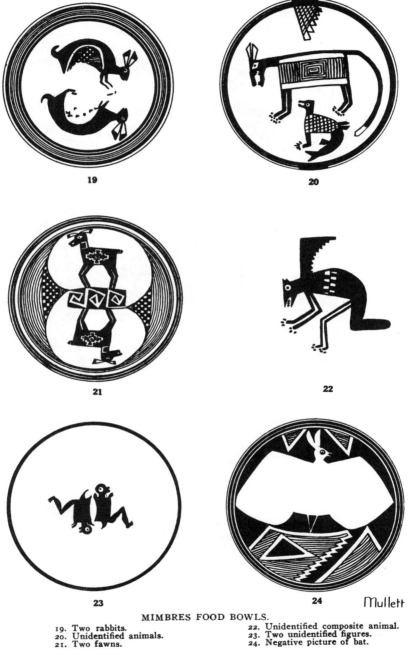

MIMBRES FOOD BOWLS.

19. Two rabbits.   22. Unidentified composite animal.
20. Unidentified animals.   23. Two unidentified figures.
21. Two fawns.   24. Negative picture of bat.

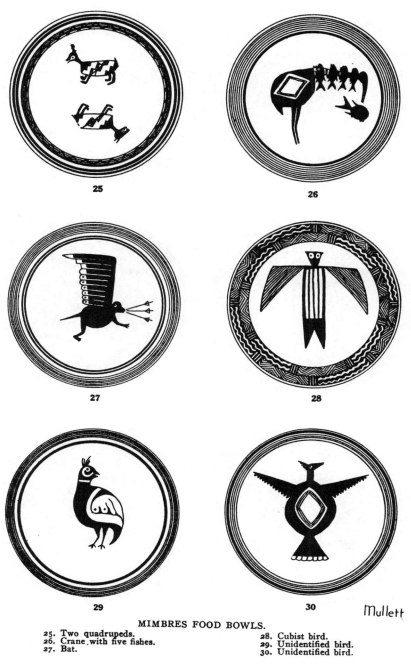

MIMBRES FOOD BOWLS.

25. Two quadrupeds.
26. Crane with five fishes.
27. Bat.

28. Cubist bird.
29. Unidentified bird.
30. Unidentified bird.

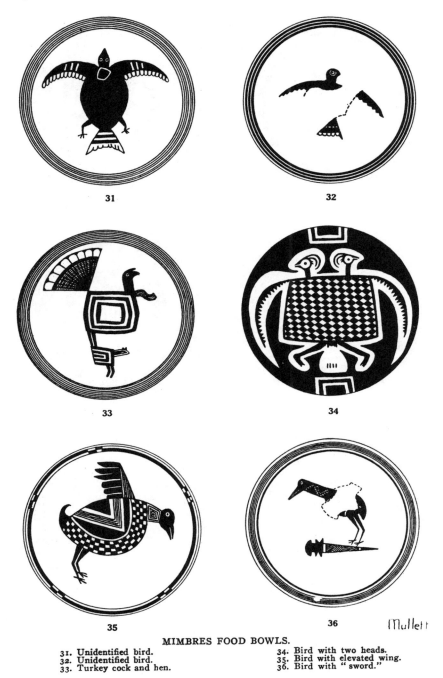

MIMBRES FOOD BOWLS.

31. Unidentified bird.
32. Unidentified bird.
33. Turkey cock and hen.

34. Bird with two heads.
35. Bird with elevated wing.
36. Bird with " sword."

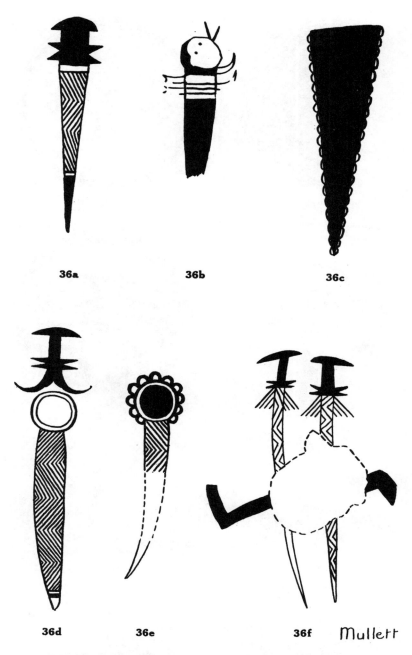

36a   36b   36c

36d   36e   36f   Mullett

UNIDENTIFIED OBJECTS FROM DIFFERENT FOOD BOWLS.

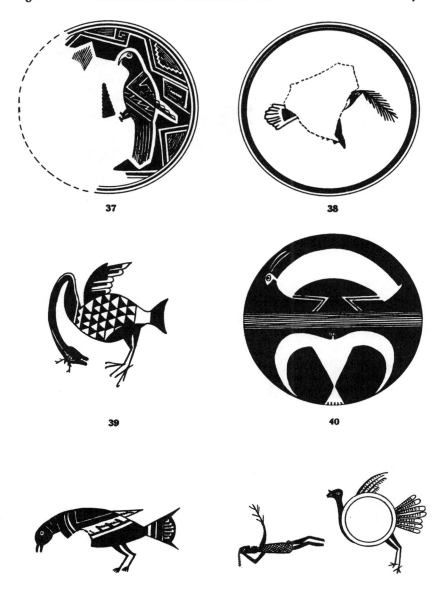

MIMBRES FOOD BOWLS.

37. Parrot.
38. Dove (?) with object in beak.
39. Unidentified bird.
40. Negative pictures of rabbit and bird.
41. Unidentified bird.
42. Man herding turkey.

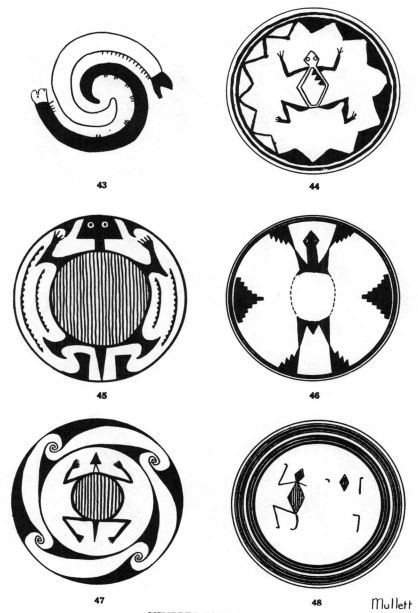

43

44

45

46

47

48   Mullett

MIMBRES FOOD BOWLS.

43. Two serpents.   46. Turtle.
44. Lizard.   47. Turtle.
45. Turtle.   48. Lizard.

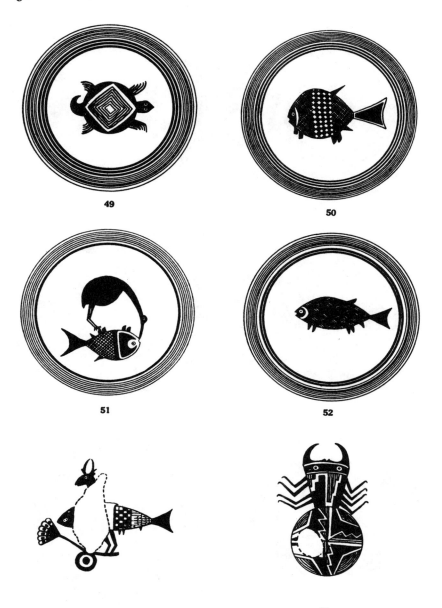

MIMBRES FOOD BOWLS.

49. Turtle.
50. Fish.
51. Bird and fish.

52. Fish.
53. Antelope, fish, and unknown object.
54. Arachnid.

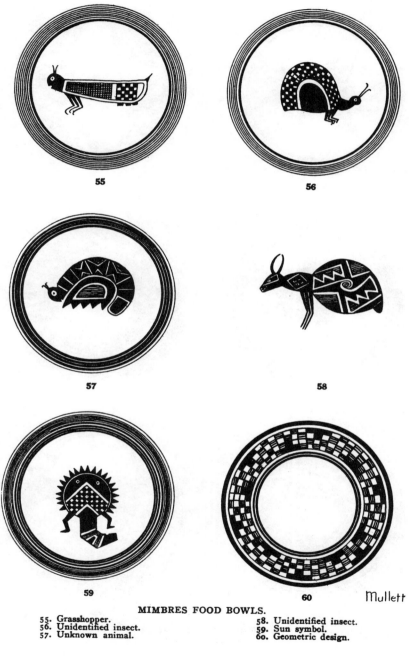

MIMBRES FOOD BOWLS.

55. Grasshopper.
56. Unidentified insect.
57. Unknown animal.

58. Unidentified insect.
59. Sun symbol.
60. Geometric design.

61   62

63   64

65   66   Mullett

MIMBRES FOOD BOWLS.
Geometric Designs.

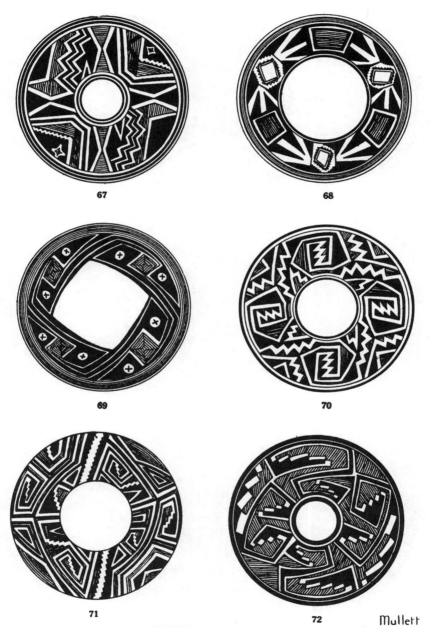

67

68

69

70

71

72   Mullett

MIMBRES FOOD BOWLS.
Geometric Designs.

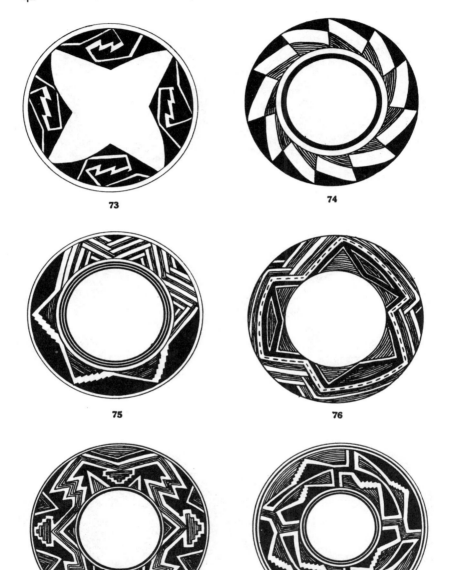

73

74

75

76

77

78

Mullett

MIMBRES FOOD BOWLS.
Geometric Designs.

79   80

81   82

83   84   Mullett

MIMBRES FOOD BOWLS.
Geometric Designs.

85

86

87

88

89

90

Mullett

MIMBRES FOOD BOWLS.
Geometric Designs.

91   92

93   94

95   96   Mullett

MIMBRES FOOD BOWLS (FIG. 93, CLAY DISK).
Geometric Designs.

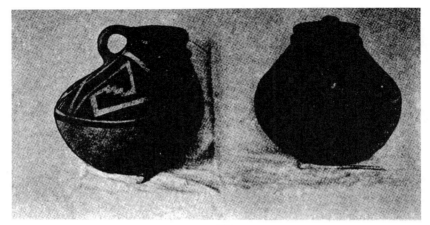

97

99   100   98

101

MIMBRES POTTERY.

97. Effigy vase (lateral and front view).	100. Unidentified insect.
98. Effigy vase (lateral view).	101. Four rough corrugated jars.
99. Mountain sheep.	

(46)

Avanyu Publishing Inc.

Other Titles Available

Heart of the Dragonfly *by Allison Bird.* This work discusses the development and history of the cross necklaces worn and made by the Pueblo Indians of New Mexico and Arizona and the Navajo Indians. The book is filled with historic photographs showing Indians wearing cross necklaces in social and ceremonial settings. 208 pages; 8 color plates; 128 black and white photos; PB, $39.95.

Moki Snake Dance *by Walter Hough PhD, Introduction by Joseph Traugott.* This travel guide originally published by the Santa Fe Railroad in 1899 describes the unparalleled drama of the Snake Dance ceremonial of the Moki (Hopi) Indians of Arizona. The easy to read narrative includes the *Snake Legend,* day-to-day descriptions of pueblo life. 80 pages; 75 black and white photos; PB, $5.95.

Style Trends of Pueblo Pottery 1500 - 1840 *by Harry P. Mera, Introduction by Jonathan Batkin.* This title reprints one of the singularly most influential works concerning Pueblo Indian pottery. This work is <u>the</u> definitive statement on historic pottery since it serves as the foundation for understanding the nomenclature and developmental sequence of Pueblo pottery. 192 pages; 67 plates; PB, $29.95.

Tusayan Katcinas and Hopi Katcina Altars *by Jesse Walter Fewkes; Introduction by Barton Wright.* Fewkes discusses the ceremonials of the Tusayan (Hopi) Indians and the Cibola (Zuni) Indians, describing their more important rituals as well as the secret **kiva** katcina altars of the Hopi. 120 pages; 18 black and white illustrations; 8 color plates; PB; $17.95.

The Mimbres, Art and Archaeology *by Jesse Walter Fewkes; Introduction by J.J. Brody.* The insightful overview provided by noted Mimbres authority, J.J. Brody, introduces the original research and writings done between 1914 and 1934 by noted ethnographer, J.W. Fewkes. 182 pages, **300+** illustrations; HB $29.95, PB, $16.95.

Petroglyphs and Pueblo Myths of the Rio Grande *by Carol Patterson-Rudolph.* Rudolph in this new work not only describes individual rock art symbols but also focuses on their meaning within the context of a language system. The book explains that the petroglyph symbols actually relate stories and myths which continue to the present among Pueblo Indian people. 160 pages; 61 black and white photos; 9 color plates; PB, $29.95.

Nacimientos *by Guy and Doris Monthan.* This revised edition of the 1979 classic displays the works of 17 New Mexico and Arizona artists and traces the 2000 year history of the Christmas nativity scene. Text in English, German, Spanish. 108 pages, 38 color plates; PB, $29.95.

Tonita Pena *by Samuel Gray.* Biography of the remarkably talented first **female** Pueblo Indian painter from Cochiti Pueblo, NM, including memoirs from her family and friends. 96 pages, 43 color plates, 9 black and white plates; HB, $39.95, PB, $29.95.

Hopi Snake Ceremonies *by Jesse Walter Fewkes.* Reprints of two essays dating from 1894 and 1897 describing and picturing in detail this most famous and spectacular Indian ceremony. The ceremony has been closed to non-Indians since 1986. 160 pages, 51 black and white plates; PB, $16.95.

A Little History of the Navajos *by Oscar H. Lipps.* This concise, authentic, and comprehensive history of the Navajo Indians of the Southwest was originally printed in 1909. It provides a first-hand view of the Navajo by a man who lived among them for years. 136 pages, 16 black and white plates; HB $19.95.

J. B. Moore, United States Licensed Indian Trader *Introduction by Marian Rodee.* Reprints of all catalogs and flyers issued by Moore from his trading post on the Navajo Reservation dating from 1903 to 1911, depicting fine Navajo rugs, ceremonial baskets, jewelry, silverware and curios. 120 pages, 30 color plates, 32 black and white photos; PB, $16.50.

C. N. Cotton and His Navajo Blankets *by Lester L. Williams, M.D.* Biography of the premier Navajo trader, blanket dealer, and frontier entrepreneur from Gallup, N.M.; the volume includes reprints of the first mail order catalogs printed to market Navajo blankets dating from 1896. 102 pages, 13 color plates, 48 black and white plates, PB, $22.50.

Zuni Fetishism *by Ruth Kirk.* Kirk describes the homes of the fetishes of the Zuni Indians of New Mexico and their position in Zuni religion and ceremony based on her studies of 25 pieces at the Museum of New Mexico. 72 pages, 10 black and white plates; PB, $4.75.

Zuni Indians *by Matilda Coxe Stevenson.* The Twenty-Third Annual Report of the Bureau of American Ethnology, 1901-1902, which describes in detail the life, customs, ceremonies, religion, kachinas, arts and crafts of these reticent western New Mexico pueblo Indians. 648 pages; 125 black and white illustrations; 48 color plates. $50.00.

Zuni Katcinas, An Analytical Study *By Ruth Bunzel.* The Forty-Seventh Annual Report of the Bureau of American Ethnology, 1929-1930. This exhaustive study has long been considered the only authoritative report on the religion and mythology of these isolated and secretive New Mexico Indians. 272 pages. HB, $30.00.

Shipping charges will be additional.

P.O. Box 27134 • Albuquerque, New Mexico 87125 • (505) 243-8485 • (505) 266-6128